THE
COLLECTED POEMS
OF
ROSE
DRACHLER

THE
COLLECTED POEMS
OF
ROSE
DRACHLER

ASSEMBLING PRESS
NEW YORK
1983

Hardbound ISBN 0-915066-49-5
Paper ISBN 0-915066-50-4

Some of Rose Drachler's work has previously appeared in the
following periodicals: *Abraxas, Alcatraz, Choice, Contact II,
European Judaism, Hand Book, The Helen Review, Invisible
City, Junction, La Fusta, Minnesota Review, The Montclair
Journal, New Wilderness Letter, New York Quarterly, New York
Times, Small Press Review, Tree, Unmuzzled Ox, Wind, Zone.*

Assembling Press
P.O. Box 1967
Brooklyn Station
Brooklyn, NY 11202

DESIGN BY BLIEM KERN
Typeset by Ed Hogan/Aspect Composition
13 Robinson St., Somerville, Mass. 02145

Editor's Note

The texts and titles of these poems are given exactly as the poet prepared them for publication. In this respect, there has been no editing. All the poems of her first two books are included here. During the last few years of her life, Rose had compiled for submission to publishers several manuscript collections, two of which were variant versions of a Recent Poems, and two were versions of a Selected Poems. When it became clear to me after her death that only a Collected Poems would suffice as a final book, I used her projected collections as a guide for the additional inclusions. I believe the canon is reasonably complete.

The grouping of poems in six sections follows a combined strategy of theme, genre and chronology. Within each section, the order is chronological in reverse, leading off with the most recent poems. As an overture at the head of each section, we print extracts from a journal which the poet kept from 1979 to 1982. These prose selections are intended not so much to introduce the poems as to reveal the poet herself working through the daily flux of concerns which later lead into the transformations of poems.

The book begins with major examples of her lyrical or meditative poems. The second group of poems, mainly autobiographical, deals with love, marriage, family and friendship. The third and largest section of the book shows Rose's central preoccupation with Jewish texts and traditions, Jewish faith and fate. The next group of poems shows the poet's deep involvement with our ancient earth and all its creatures. Section Five might be entitled Translations and Conversations, revealing Rose's intellectual engagement with other poets, thinkers and artists, either by way of actual translations or by communions of the spirit, in which texts are adapted and transmuted. The poems of the final section explore nightmare realms of disorder and confusion, of the uncanny and unruly forces loose in the world and in man.

Rose Drachler died July 10, 1982. She was 71, and had been writing seriously for the last twenty years of her life. Her first book, *Burrowing In, Digging Out* (1974) represented the exciting period of discovering herself as a poet. The next period brought her the suffering of cancer surgery and chemotherapy, and the enormous lift of studying with John Ashbery. It resulted in an even stronger book, *The Choice* (1977). The work of the last five years, which appears here in book form for the first time, is clearly of a new depth. Now readers can view the entire body of her work in perspective. It was a truly inspired achievement, carried out with unflinching integrity.

7

I would like to express here—as Rose Drachler often did in the past—our feelings of happiness and gratitude to the circle of young friends, poets and artists, who gave of their fellowship and high spirits to dispel our sometimes nagging sense of isolation:

Michael Andre, Rae Berolzheimer, Elizabeth Cook, Moira Crone, Charles Doria, Barbara Einzig, Marcia Falk, Dorothy Friedman, Rodger Kamenetz, Maurice Kenny, Jackson Mac Low, David Meltzer, Susan Mernit, Charlie Morrow, Rochelle Ratner, Armand Schwerner, Erika Rothenberg, Carol Rubenstein, Diane and Jerome Rothenberg, Ann Tardos, Nina Yankowitz, John Yau.

It would be impossible to detail here the individual graces that each of them contributed to Rose's life and mine, but I must give warmest special thanks to Charles Doria, who acted as publisher, for his unstinting labors in bringing this book to a timely and beautiful launching. I am also deeply grateful to Rochelle Ratner for her editorial acumen in helping shape the final structure of this volume.

Jacob Drachler

Books

Burrowing In, Digging Out, TREE, Berkeley, 1974
The Choice, TREE, Berkeley, 1977
Eight on Eight, GRIDGRAFFITI, Brooklyn, 1977
Amulet Against Drought, TIDELINE PRESS, Tannersville, N.Y., 1978
For Witches, BLACK MESA PRESS, Madison, Wisconsin, 1982

Anthologies

in *A Big Jewish Book*, edited by Jerome Rothenberg with Harris Lenowitz and Charles Doria, ANCHOR PRESS/DOUBLEDAY, New York, 1978
in *Voices Within the Ark*, edited by Howard Schwartz and Anthony Rudolf, AVON BOOKS, New York, 1980

Award

Received *The American Book Award* 1981 from The Before Columbus Foundation.

PREFACE

"I give you an apple," she writes, "where we stand / at the center" & points, in saying so, to the wonder of these poems. Because hers is a centered work: the work of a woman alive in her language & in the sense of where that language comes from. This accounts too for the work's mystery, which is the mystery of a tradition absorbed & issuing in sharp components, assemblages of sensory & intellectual data (perceptions) whose orders & music ring true. She is a genuine kabbalist: a poet whose work is totally comprehensible—& totally mysterious.

So her book—like all poem-books since Whitman brought the message home—is the life, the song of herself created in the work. "My own," she says, "I do not conceal / Or deny what I am": a Jewish woman into her late 60s who is a Jewish woman into her late 60s: who has been (for how long?) like those secret wise men in each generation, one of the 36 poets whose work stays hidden in the world.

But time is so crazy, so unreal at last, that it presents her to us now & we realize our loss at not having sooner been informed. Her work appeared to me first in David Meltzer's magazine, *Tree*, a poem with an almost Stein-like clarity, in which she counted numbers:

One
One and one
Two
Two and one
Four horns
Corners
One and seven he counted
One and six

& I could hear in that the numbers counted by the letter-&-number poets of Jewish mysticism: the numbers counted off as "omer" & "to make the corners right." This was her meditation, then, which she permitted us to share, as in other poems we shared the moments of her life in dream & waking, other languages: Yiddish, Latin, Sumerian, Egyptian.

I'm eager, anyway, to welcome her. The voice is quiet, not insistent, yet the poet's wildness sounds beneath it. Maybe the poet's fire, which is very bright here & which lets us see the darkness of the world.

Jerome Rothenberg

9

TABLE OF CONTENTS

IV

V

VI

I

October 21, 1979

I was going through my mother's things after she died and I came across a diary. There were very short entries for each day. "Today is a clear day. The sun is shining." That sort of thing, nothing from inside of herself, no interesting occurrences. More than anything about her long-drawn-out pain and death, the final weeks of yelping and howling like a pup that has been run over, more than that, this broke me up and I keep recalling it. She had an empty life. She married, to get out of an insufferable position, a man twenty one years older than herself, who was rich and respected. She paid for her lack of courage with everything. Except a relationship, very close, it is true, with the sea and the weather. "The ocean is lovely today, clean and calm. I enjoyed my swim very much."

For almost a year now I have had a struggle with writing. When I plan to write something, dig up an idea or group of phrases with which I might work up a poem, my own censor sits behind me and suggests that it is not worth doing. The idea has no merit. The phrases are neither new nor worth the labor. The inability to write is a kind of sneeze which will not let go. I am very troubled. Some relief, I do get, from writing letters to people whom I revere from a distance, not having any real relationship with them at all. It reminds me of Longfellow's poem which we had to put to memory when I was a child in school; "I shot an arrow into the air. It fell to earth I know not where." If my mother with her empty days could keep a diary, most of the pages of which were empty to suit her perception of her place and accomplishments, I can make that effort and write, at least to that extent.

I do not think that I write for honor, although there is some question about that. Perhaps beneath the surface, where I have these vain longings. Yes, certainly such feelings are there, or were. Why do I try so hard to get published from time to time? But then I draw back and try to be a private person, serving my family and friends and just writing as a kind of compulsion, when the fit is on me. A fit it is. My eyes are not focused on those around me, if they should address me, and I take a long time to respond to the ringing of the phone or doorbell, not because I do not hear it exactly but because I hear as if through a wall, from a distance. How I long for that spell to come over me. When I am writing, it seems nothing too long for so, a perfectly ordinary thing, *my* thing. This, then, is day one of my diary and it may have pages on which I shall write, "The sun is shining."

December 14, 1979

I am beginning to read a book which we received from the Princeton U. Press yesterday. THE INNER THEATER OF RECENT FRENCH POETRY by Mary Ann Caws. It is a good choice. I knew it would be. Like conversation with a friend who is like me but very much my superior. For me, her writing is a kind of stretching of my faculties and fills my head with the best kind of "high thought", not necessarily on the subject under discussion. She is particularly interested in motion and not-motion as shown in the poetry of Cendrars, Tzara, Peret, Artaud and Bonnefoy, all of whom I am unfamiliar with. I am particularly interested in silence. When I write poetry I start with three or so pages and work back to less and less of a statement, trying to include the spirit of what I wrote, in as small a compass as is possible, using the quietest words or no words at all. The reading of such work would require a certain kind of reader.

A line of Caws' words, a paragraph, sends me into my main thoughts: About dying, what it means, how best to do it, About time, the way it all exists at once. That, if a person has a heart, for example, and the heart beats, it is like the ticking of a clock and there is the beat BEFORE and the beat AFTER, so that for us there is a beginning and an end and the progress toward the end of time: In our consciousness only, because looked at from far enough away all the beats, all the ticking is taking place in one space of time. It is the old story of the river. There is the source of the river, high in the hills and small; then there is the substance of the river dispersed in separate drops out at sea. It happens all at once. It is *rivering.* To be a river includes it all, the beginning and the end; And with it all, there is not a beginning or an end because there are clouds and rain drops and snow which are an earlier part of the river and there are sea-creatures, icebergs etc. which are a later part of the river. Earlier and later being part of a simultaneous process. So with my death, which I study almost all the time now, and really for no reason except that I like to do a thing bravely and well, like making love, I would like to get whatever is possibly in it, out of it.

February 4, 1980

I come on too Jewish with these people who are not Jewish. It makes that a sort of frame in which I enclose myself, so then they do that too—which I dislike a little. Yes, I am. But what else am I? Anything? Or no?

I was voted the most eccentric girl in a college of six thousand girls, most of whom were Jewish. So it was not particularly my Jewishness. There is some other quality which the girls considered unusual. I flatter myself that it was an urgency toward truth, the bottom truth in acts and relationships. (I do not like that word, *relationships*.)

There always is a solution to any problem. The girls in my classes did not consider my solutions acceptable. They *worked* for me. The food I ate when I had no money. The clothes I wore to school since I had no others. The strings of beads I wore made from seeds and bones. That my hair was long, worn *a bonne femme*, and nobody did that then. If you keep your habits long enough, eventually they become stylish and acceptable.

Even if you are not in style, by the time you get old, people are used to your ways. I am old.

February 22, 1980

I have struggled with the French poem assignment Ashbery handed out to his workshop, where I audited the class about ten days ago and come up with a poem of sorts. It is not what I admire in my own work, in fact it is not my own work, but it is a poem and I would not have written it without the goad of the assignment. What I do is follow the SOUNDS of the French, not the meaning—which I could discern if I preferred. It is like what Zukofsky did with Catullus, but I make a poem of my own with it.

The strange thing is that working so hard at sounds to struggle through to meanings, I find ideas in my work of which I neither approve nor consider part of my self. It is always surprising to me to find these sour, shallow, even meretricious under-currents peeking out from my well disciplined subconscious. I do not approve of my hidden nature. It is not a person I would choose for a lifelong friend, but as they say in Hebrew, *Ain Breirah* —there is no choice. No alternative would be a better translation, perhaps. Of course I can work this stranger out of the poem —I do try to—or discard the poem once it is finished, and I often do, but it represents so much effort that it takes time for me to get to it. Once the poem is what I call finished I can hardly find the sounds that brought it about in the original French poem.

It would be useful to keep the many steps toward the final work. They say Ezra Pound did this with his "Chinese" translations, and some other poets also. I tried it on my own years ago with *More Rays*, not one of my best poems either.

The way I prefer to write a poem is to have a phrase begin to sound in my head, to follow through with an idea or story based on that phrase and not to put the poem down on paper until it says itself right off from my silent work within. I call this a GIVEN poem. Usually it is better than the ones I rewrite dozens of times or so I feel when I write it. Later some of the most difficult and re-written things stand firmer, with more to them. In any case the poems I wrote while with the workshop were foreign to me in a disturbing way. Not *I* spoke them. Another. Perhaps the teacher? Is it better not to write at all rather than to be seduced into ideas so antipathetic to everything one aims at? I do need to write.

February 10, 1982

So now what? The biopsy was positive. I have carcinoma in various parts of my body and acytes, a disfunctioning accumulation of fluid in the abdomen. It causes me not to be able to eat more than a few tablespoonsful of food or liquid and I have trouble breathing.

Before I went into the hospital for this I had a beautiful dream. I dreamt that I awakened in the night. The curtains were drawn aside and I could see the moon above my two dear spruce trees. The face of the moon was totally covered by a black dish with an irregular crack running more than halfway across it. Through the crack and around the edges the brilliant light of the moon could be seen. The whole sky, besides was full of a milky mist of moonlight. I was delighted to see this and turned to Jacob—in my dream — to awaken him, so we could share this strange, beautiful sight. Jacob was breathing noisily in his sleep, having difficulty continuing to sleep. He is not a good sleeper. I thought about what I was looking at with deep contentment and continued to sleep with no other dreams. In the morning I remembered the dream very plain. I knew then that it was a death dream which I could not share and I wept because the moon, Hekate, which has always been very helpful to me had its face covered, except for that irregular crack. And her dogs, Hekate's dogs, would be tearing me apart soon. Soon.

In the hospital, Friday night, I had an episode of being unable to breathe. It frightened me of course, but most of all I was in despair because water, the first love of my life, my home, my comfort, since I swam in amniotic fluid before I was born — and recall it ever since, my ocean besides which I always live to look at it, smell it, float in it. It turns on me. Becomes my killer.

We all die of something, air, or water or moonlight. I would like to present a spartan face to my family. But the disappointments are, step by step, inch by inch, abandonment, treachery in the most basic sense.

When Nina was small I used to lose my patience, then my temper, and I would beat. She would then climb up into my lap, weeping, and say, "Mommy, I hurt myself."

I feel that way now. What, no air? Too much water? The moon, my sister, my bad midwife. My matchmaker, — from me? All gone.

21

ENTRANCE TO THE APPLE ORCHARD

Turn on the faucet and wet everything with its own name
We stand facing the thing as we name it. Cornice
The cornice runs all around the inside of the building
A horizon under the glass dome. Dome

The light beneath which we stand
In the center under the dome
Is more pure than under the skies
Outside of the building

The building has fluted pilasters
Stone apples, balustrades carved
Into leafy branches, lanterns
Of stone toward which all lines
Of sight are drawn

What is the use of all this language
All this variety?
We need stones as they come out
Of the earth. No hierarchies, no gradations

> I give you an apple where we stand
> At the center. *Tapooakh. Malus*
> It is white fleshed
> Streaked with pink, crisp and wet
> Under your teeth, clear, winy
> To your tongue. It smells a bit like
> Roseleaves on a sunlit morning
>
> I name an apple, a plain stone, a light
> Under a dome where we have stood
> Looking up for almost fifty years
> Unmarked by a name. Care, I name it
> Love. My love. Hands, I name it

We face each other and give names
To absent things long gone
The name, although it is not the thing
Is necessary
To the thing itself and to us

We are not to be heavy-hearted
Now that almost everything has its name
Others that stood under this tight light
Before us, gave other names

We name this spot *the end of naming*
Earlier visitors said it was
The *entrance to the apple orchard*
Later visitors may come here
And call it the *exit*

THE SIGNS, THE WORDS

Lamb, cooked, is food to the man
Lamb, running, is food for the jaguar
"Lamb is a person. Not food." says the jaguar's wife

      The man, the jaguar and the jaguar's wife
      Share the same signs and words

      The man, disemboweled, appears in the sky
      As a group of stars, shining

      The wife transformed for thinking odd thoughts
      Becomes water, becomes now the man's wife
      In her, fish live, lilies float
      Hibiscus grows, the amiable manatee grazes

      In a dry time she can be found in melons
      A container contained

      Theirs is a union of strange pairs
      Starlight plus earth-water

      The births they make mediate between them
      They bring forth new creatures
      Bright plumaged birds shining with starlight
      Shimmering like water

I touch my mouth. I'm hungry
Or thirsty. "Water." I say
You know about thirst
You know the sign, the word
You give me water

But there is only difference between us
"Lamb." you say, and lick your lips
"Clouds." I dream, and picture lambs
Leaping straight up
The signs, the words, are the same
For us both

THIRST

Three women are imprisoned in a room with no doors or windows
They are cared for, fed, given water
One woman looks for a way out
The others sit and watch her
They are finished with trying
One drinks a glass of water in gulps
The water runs down her chin
She remains thirsty

A young Africaans family pares thin strips of venison off
    a flayed deer
They are making THIRSTY MEAT
The children help. They love this meat. They enjoy making it
The pretty blond mother and her fair sons smile
The kitchen shed in which they work is dim
Outdoors the sunlight is very strong

The mother looks in the mirror
She sees not herself but a Bantu man
With the flayed carcass of a woman on his back
The carcass is heavy. The sun is hot
The man is thirsty. He is carrying what makes him thirsty

EQUAL GIFTS

The twelve top men, the princes
Gave twelve great gifts
Equal in number, in size exactly
They did not wish to outdo each other

Twelve solid gold spoons
Full of incense, very dear
Twelve silver bowls
Full of fine white flour
Twelve white horses
With waving white tails

The people without number
Gave twelve dear parts of themselves
The heart, the stomach, the gullet
The palate, the guts, the face
The liver, the kidneys, the spleen
The hands, the eyes, the back

       "Losses," she said quietly
       With a small deprecating smile
       "Losses," sitting blind in the nursing home
       Patient, with less laughter
       Now that sitting was all
       That was required of her

       She had sent her man to America
       To save himself

With whatever remained in the house
She had baked and cooked
And gone to the market to sell
Leaving the children crying
For a taste of good round breads

She found a rich peasant
Who gave her a hut rent-free

And what else?
Twelve years later her man
Sent for them from America
A smooth pious man

The gifts were exactly equal
So many bowls, so many spoons
So many losses, so many years
The years adding up to the same
As the years that have passed
Since creation

HOUSEWORK, AN ASYLUM

*"If the room/ cell becomes the confines of the light/
energy of the mind, the open wall points to the future
beyond the self . . . to no mind or one mind. ASYLUM
becomes a gateway to a specific kind of freedom
available to those who open the right door."*
                                                    Owen Morrel

When she was a child she would slide her hands
palms up, under her scapulae, lifting them
away from her back like wings. "Wings," she
would say, "Wings." But with time and the

countless repetitions of doing what was needed
every day, one foot in front of the other
her hands pulling, twisting, or lifting,
wings were not necessary. The sky was closed

but it was as porous as atomic particles.
Air blew through it. That other air blew through
and her other self rose up like smoke and
passed through as if it were open.

Within herself each part was free, although
it did what was expected. The feet were free
to go or to return. She wore paths down
to where anyone could tell where the path

went through the wall as each day lay down
in front of her feet like an old saying. "This
is how it went before. This is how it goes now.
So it will go as long as the feet go."

Her mouth was full of song. The song was inside
even when she was quiet. She chose these limits
for the freedom it gave her. The expected is a
kind of sleep within which something essential

is always dreaming. Anything new or refreshing
is inimical. It hinders the ease of the habitual.
She returned to the customary for comfort.
The tedium was medicinal. It was an ease

sought by the limbs and parts, like sleep.
The way of being almost asleep is
surrounded by a wide soft air. Another path
other work, like but unlike, always took place

to either side and above the measured placing
of one foot in front of the other on the
worn down path. To say that she was free
or not free, was to talk another language

a language in which such things were not possible.
She had other lives going all the time.
It was not just this life or that one.
It was not just awake and compelled, or asleep

and free. There were other places and ways
to be in them. They were easy to find, to inhabit.
Even the place where work set by others
had to be done day by day. The work was a grid
through which she passed into those other places
singing snatches of song. She sang to herself.
The song was from here but it was for there.
That was the point. No one accompanied her

where she rose like a vapor through the wall
or the closed door with ease. The color of that place
where she rose alone was orange-yellow.
It was like the inside of a flower for a bee.

THE END OF HER VERSE

(for Amy Goldin)

In that country, to make pictures of real creatures is against the rule so there are no pictures of animals, people or flowers except when the artist-craftsman needs to break the rule and even then the picture is enclosed by a tight barrier, a compartment or rectangle, and when the princess leans out of her rectangle-called-window, a square must be removed from it and her head, gentle with longing is a curve, unique in that place, and must lean diagonally against all the right-angles toward her enclosed lover below, as tender as can be. There is a dragon too, closed in his own rectangle and in the center below the window is Alexander on his famous horse, Bucephalus, squarely separated by his history. Nothing is not restrained by straight lines, even the calligraphy, all around the edges like a frame, a page within the page, is squared off with right angles implicit and absolute.

All is lavish with gold. The lettering is blue because she was "a good tree with root firm and branches in heaven" which is very blue in that place too.

There are blades of grass or rose petals, even, that can break stone, so the small rosettes and palmettes break through the lines of the rigid barriers in places. The oriental mind, they say, is stable and fanatical, and Amy, small Amy, with her barrier-breaking mind became an art critic. She won prizes before she died.

The dragon was not restrained by his compartment in the gold rectangle. The story tells that he did break out and get the princess leaning her curved head in the square-removed-from-the-rectangle.

She had more life than could be contained within a rectangle of a page painted on a page. I mark the breaking of her barrier, the end of her verse, half-real, half-imaginary abstract, painted like a manuscript with illuminations in gold and blue, adorned like fine metal work, as intricate, yet simple, as a floral rug made in Persia.

She had an oriental mind, stable and fanatical, a grid on which the calligraphy of "people strange to her people" broke through in tenderness in spite of precedent and habit. All the proportions of her mind and thought were balanced neatly, so many horizontal, so many vertical all in gold and blue, that special blue, with the relief of the diagonal position of her sweet head leaning in tenderness toward what was outside the frame of the rectangle.

MARRIAGE

There are two crude forces arrayed against each other
They elongate, flatten, coil, are notched at the edges
They create a plausibility of daily, hourly insistence

Two on a combined axis are more than their geometries
They are balanced all around with a visceral hump
Together they become vestigial, larval, antique

One muscle always begins to pull before the other
Thus they rid themselves of their mutuality
They lift, retract, breathe. They protect one another

The whole story may be read in the aperture
Through which the union takes place
Through it they converge. They pull away from it

It is a pull that goes up. It goes down
It goes straight on into each other
It grows back into itself like a rodent's tooth

Viewed from outside or above nothing is happening
But they clamp. The other half becomes the parent
Becomes a mirror image. They are sealed

They only seem sluggish, immobile through life
Always between the two parts is an imbalance
They drag. They topple. They fall over

The more ornate their habitat, the higher their spire
The more they tend to topple over. They pull away. They cling
A whirling of air and earth surrounds this struggle

The imbalance curves them. They become circular
They coil on themselves. They conceal the place
Because they are in a mantle together, tied, they drag

Like a sack-race, a three-legged race, they hop or leap
They are scarred where they join. They are awkward
An extinct form, crawling as in a cage of bones

THE CAUSA IMMANENS

"What is the Matter?"
Matter is the template
against which
I shape myself.

A living universe not
intelligent, particularly.
My necessity is true freedom
but I enslave myself
to you and others.

Slavery is my choice so I am free.
I stand between the world of matter
and a unity apart from things,
a broom in my hand and a potato
which I cook to
realize myself.

"Is something the Matter?"
Yes. The Spirit in Things, the one
and only principle, what is in
me, in a broom, in a potato
the beginning, the middle
and the end of us all.

LABYRINTH

Where what THE is, is the secret of the doctor who posits the THE
The door to identity is the theater of heroes.

Since man lives life as a hymn to nature and life is a city
So the city and life equal a homeplace for man and his hymn.

The role of the hero separates, takes away the hymn.
Where the hero makes nothing of man who needs mystery?

The hymn is maternal, no one believes in it now.
Measure the opening of the door to see if the space will suffice.

The narrowness of the door is not a problem, since what
   is abortable
What refuses solitude is secret, which abrogates the idea
   of solitude.

The time has come to climb above these faults
Which unroll themselves with flashes of intense pain.

Her son will be a hero. Bring him to her.
Hymn her hidden treasure. The door is shut for the time being.

The figleaf is for the doctor. Before this leaf was found
He said, "Place the two leaves where they can be

A modest concealment of first causes." The generations follow
As summer follows spring and can be reproduced

Exactly in the door through which the doctor enters.
In the works these leaves were brightened as with crayon.

The doctor brings a double identity.
If this equals that, then that also equals this.

As an idea is a hymn, a hero being an idea is a hymn also,
Since the hero equals the hymn and the doctor equals
   the mystery

Mystery being an idea, the doctor and the hero equal one unit.
Therefore this proves that the doctor may enter the door
   in another form.

The doctor IS the door. The door is a narrow box. The box
   is a mystery.
The hero is a hymn and a door to death. Since life is the doctor's

And the city is life there is a solution. It is not normal.
The doctor is the Father. He is not pleased.

He demands a clear picture. He denies the mystery. Money. Work.
Appointments. Dressed up in love and ideas leave by
   the front door.

Call him when you are fulgurating.

I DREAM OF AIR

I always love shoes
to come in twos
and look like feet
from a different country
where people are honest,

thick soft leather
grey or oatmeal color
never shined, edible-looking.

In my dream I find
such a shoe in a store
There is no pair, one only.

I pick up my feet
and lie down on the air
at the height of the counter.

The one shoe I carry
bursts into flames
as I swim slowly away on air.

It is difficult
to swim through the air.
I long for the mate
of the shoe from my
unknown home country.

"The soul puts on
its shoes. The soul
ties its shoes."

I am homesick for the air
of my home country.

JOY IN THE DESERT

I breathe lions at two A.M.
I am up yours Lord
Lord. My rainbow
I am your thorny rose

I have been eating rainbows
There are bits of rainbow
Stuck in my teeth
               O the joy of our espousals
You. Yourself. My yours
I am full of lions
Swim in pearl
           when I followed you in the desert
Lord, your mane is in my nose
I breathe it golden
Airy

THE EVENING OF THE SIXTH DAY

A Fugue for Tina Meltzer

I search for not knowing in the middle of what I know best.
This is a bottomless well of the inconceivable
Here is the song of an unseen bird, music turned into flesh.
I reflect on my own powers. Am amazed at the familiar.

By what instrument have I reduced myself to perfection?
Here is the song of a tiny bird, music made flesh
What profound geometry. What exquisite principle.
A walnut is fashioned so like a brain. I laugh. I am afraid.

The song I hear is from an unseen bird. It is flesh made
    from music.
There is a remarkable sort of statistical dissymmetry.
I examine the spatial developments, how they relate
Nothing resembles any other thing exactly.

To say that it is accidental is to say that it exists.
I reflect on my own powers. Am amazed at the familiar.
I can describe what I see in terms of what I saw before
But changes have occurred. By reducing the scale I learn love.

This can go on indefinitely. Of this who would grow weary?
I know nothing of seashells or tiny mushrooms.
I look for the first time and am perplexed. Did I do this?
I reflect on my own powers. Am amazed at the familiar.

The idea of making or remaking is hard to take in.
My own metaphysics and science give me vertigo.
I pretend to know what I know. I go back to the
Beginning of knowing. One can discern a certain construction.

I look for the first time and am perplexed.
There is the work of someone not working at random.
I recognize his work. An unseen bird. Music made flesh.
It is the fruit of humor. A Mozart is playing jokes.

Someone made these for someone else as a partial gift.
To say that it is accidental is to say it exists.
Here is cohesion. Here is reality of matter.
I must disregard their origin and purpose and get to work.

What profound geometry. What guiding principle.

Compare these to small stones. They have something more.
Fragments suggest fragments that were joined to them.
I reflect on my own powers. Am amazed at the familiar

Would it be possible to construct all this consciously
To get the right ingredients, make a plan, proceed step by step,
A pre-existing idea guiding the execution
An idea of the work that governs its progress?

Compare these to small stones. They have something more.
They engage my wonder and make me look for a WHOLE.
I divided myself in order to create. Of what else could
    I make them?
And the final result requires unflagging attention.

I am unable to imagine such material, such attention
I cannot even make bread twice the same way.
It is as though the idea of the similar called forth
Endless similarities. I reflect on my own powers.

A thrush is singing an acrobatic song made flesh.
I did this as I lay sleeping. Or not I, someone did this in me
A pre-existing idea directed the execution.
This is surely the work of someone not working at random.
This may go on forever. Of this who would grow weary?

BIRDSONG

Birdsong birdsong
Thin as razors
Fleeting shrill
The birds unseen
Innocent as pain
Ubiquitous

> The sweat at the roots of the hair of Owuo
> Revived his victims
> Their delicious meat and bones
> Lived once more
>
> When they burned his long silken hair
> And they poured the sweat-water on him
> Death died. Owuo died
> His food lived once more
>
> When they dropped this same water
> In his eye, it opened and blinked
> Each time it blinked one died
> He lived again Owuo. Owuo lived

Oh birdsong all through the trees
Cutting the air
The birds unseen
Innocent as death
Inevitable

FOREIGNER IN A STONY COUNTRY

Bunches of grapes all dusted with flint
Silver skins thick with light
Pressing against each other
Formed by one another

Separate, surrounded by air
In space, a stranger looking for strangers
My bread made by foreigners

No grapes, no seeds, off to one side
I hear my night tongue
I seldom speak it

Disguised, speaking to earth
In the language of stones
Dropping out, joining, barking with dogs

Masked, wearing clothes like the others
I cover the windows, muffle the floors
Wake at night or rise early

Edge near a bunch full
Of the dialect of home
Fade, take on the appearance of stone
And whisper to the dark in myself

ROSES

The unborn bear down
Curled tight
And ready to howl

The dead float upward
Hands open
Hushed

Words like water
Keeping secrets
Afloat
Floating sorrows
Like seaweed

The young girl peels an onion
Weeps and weeps
And calls it a rose
Every layer the same
A rose she insists
A rose

THE SNAKE

In the morning there is no sign
But the snake has been there
The cow is dry

My father and my mother
And those that went before them
Have filled me with strength
It is all for you
But when you leave I sleep

PEARLY EVERLASTING

The sign says East
   Eden, 14 miles
   Yet the arrow points up
To a pale blue sky

Pearly Everlasting
   Skyflower
   Cool water on the rock
Live water coming down

Points up pearly ever
   Lasting laughter
   Of the completely owned
All pearly traveling up

Pearly Everlasting, Skyflower
   Cool water on the rock
   Live water melting down
Point up Pearly Ever

Lasting laughter of the
Thoroughly loved
All pearly pointing up
14 miles to the pale blue sky

CYMBALS

Cymbals or a violin,
there was a noise before I woke.
Now it shakes the air.
Only the sound
is gone.

It glows here.
It dances.

Someone has been here.
My mouth tastes sweet.

Someone has been here
and is gone.

How good.

WHEN I PUSHED YOU AWAY WEEPING

When I pushed you away weeping
why did you go?
You lie bloody.
Unformed elbows over your no eyes,
wrapped in yourself
instead of in me.

Oh inhabitants return.
Return. Inhabit me.

Who shall fill the emptiness
of this howling house?

When you floated in my sea
and the surf pounded
so it shook your sheltered flesh
what frightened you?

DROWNING TOGETHER

Swimming alone
out where the boats go
naked and warm
gently remolded
by my mother, the sea
I die to be drowned.

Swimming together
where the water is air
cradled and gentled
held by our breathing
rising and swelling
we drown to be born.

TSUNAMI

The little waters listen quietly:
There is a hum far away
Calling.
They gather, they go,
They meet:
Now quiet and listening,
They run together,
They point and scent.

There is a wave of water:
It runs quietly, fast,
It is joined, it grows
From Japan to Peru—the surface is calm.
When it breaks,
When it meets the land,
The sound fills.
The diatoms at the sea bottom quiver.

The wave stands up
Opens its jaws
And pauses,
Leaps over the sand
To the cities,
Slavers and growls:
It eats.

Now the waters go back,
They go home:
First the big wave
With Valparaiso in its belly,
Hawaii, Anchorage,
Back to Japan, to New Zealand,
Back sated
Full.
It will return.
The little waters tumble back,
They gather again and return,
They listen and remember.

NOW LIKE A SHELTER

Now like a shelter
I stand between
cutting frost and the broad leafed evergreens
sparing them rightful pruning
by timely element
who once open mouthed
bit frost or wind sent
as trial to my young growth
as a wind screen
or a concave wing
try to shield the suneaters
at my roots
who grown thick as winter pelt
lean against the hill
and guard their tender future
which holds an axe
for me.

HOMESICKNESS

The green finch with her hair-thin claws
and her beak sharpened on a branch

falls upward, light as the night breeze.
She picks holes in the silk of the sky.

There is starlight. There are stars.

The butter-colored finch, warm in the salt air
of night's blouse, rests safe between soft moons.

Her heart beats fast. She finds pearls
at the edge of the moon. She picks them

as easily as white bugs or bread crumbs.
She has picked the edge away tonight.

There is milklight. There is moonlight.
I long for the salt air of my home.

February 11, 1980 [Her birthday]

Jacob is feeling a kind of headiness lately. He is spending lots of money. In gratitude for our still being together after four years of my insecure health. In fact I think I have been strong right through the whole ordeal. Being strong is my bottom nature, even strongly-sick. I do love my backyard, the spruces in the sunlight, the birds, the squirrels, the cats. It is something I have always felt I would regret having to leave.

My mother used to talk about the birch trees of her home in the forests of the Pripet Marshes in Russia, of gathering blueberries and picking wildflowers. A lovely world, yes. But just as leaving the lovely prebirth womb for the air of the world can only be considered in the light of increase of function, of experience and trial, so I think dying may lead to another increase.

I do not refer to HEAVEN. That is a metaphor for something much more complicated and much more simple too. Something wider, more diffused is to happen to us after death. When I first was sick and was told of the statistical chances I had of dying soon, I tried to think through what dying would mean to me. First of all I would like to do it well as it sets an example for those who are dear to me who must do the same thing in the future. Far future, I hope.

But besides all that I always like to know what will be required of me. If it is to be difficult I want to be prepared, to work with it not against it. There was an elation I felt with the imminence. That elation is gone for the last year. It will creep up on me. It will not come announced as I thought—was given to think.

How happy I am. What a charge washes through me of caring for people and of being cared for by them. Yesterday I brought John Ashbery two coverlets. They are not in the best shape. One is over two hundred years old. I mended and washed it carefully. The other is just patchwork of rectangles made in a sort of staircase pattern. The materials are old, washed pale, old-fashioned fabrics, mostly shirting, but with navy and dark red patches here and there. I love the oldness of these things, the use they have seen. But I think they may not be pleasing?

March 4, 1980

I see with amazement that people happily come all the way out here to see us. That is what it is all about anyhow, the people. I love that. In my old age. Such a blessing. My feet are light, a contentment washes over me. I sing Yiddish folksongs. "Where were you when I was young and lively and my dowry waited on the table?"

March 15, 1980

A number of women, anti-religious people, have said to me in a kind of taunting way, "How is it or isn't it true that, every morning the men say their prayers, 'Thank G-d I'm not a woman.'? But as I read it they thank G-d they are not this and not that, ending with "Thank G-d for not making me a woman" while a woman has her prayer, which is Blessed be etc. for making me the way I am. This feels much more natural and womanlike to me. I'm thankful for being a human being on this beautiful planet. I thank also for being old, a woman, a Jew. I get this good feeling, often for living here near the sea, for living at all, and certainly for being a man,, meaning human, not a starling for example, division, woman. Partly this is due to having brushed with death. I feel triumph. The sky is bluer, the air is truer. I love the trees and especially the water which surrounds the place where my house is. Not fashionable.

I remember when I had a lot of pain due to tendonitis and the doctor prescribed *indocin*, I refused to continue taking it because that feeling of buoyancy deserted me. I told the doctor I preferred the pain with this great flush of joy to being without pain and tied to my heavy feet. He looked understanding, even approving. I did not know the side effects of that drug but there must have been some acknowledged side effect that he recognized.

I'm glad I'm a woman but I can certainly not fault a man for being thankful that he is not—all things considered. I am womanly, not a feminist. Men should be made to feel strong, competent and better, because they are not, and they need to feel that they are in order to function as men. Once I said that to a class of Chinese girls, when I told about being the third daughter in four years, born to a man who divorced his first wife and married my mother to have sons.

April 20, 1980

How wonderful people are altogether. We saw, one time, on the line in the supermarket, a plainly beautiful brown-skin woman, with strong features and an enduring, honest look. She bought well too. So many people fill their shopping carts with treats, instant foods, cat-food and other non-considered uses of their limited funds. She had foods which would take work and knowledge to prepare but were taking her money much further in the long run. A soft-looking, tall, lighter-skinned, man with an earring in one ear—who worked in the supermarket—came and tried to make a date with her. He was after a more permanent connection. That was obvious. He joked, teased, looked boyishly winning. She could not help smiling, although she was a sober type and tried to keep her face unresponsive, her lips would part in a smile, her teeth flash and I got a hint of how she would be if she did not have to be so thrifty with her responses. She remained unresponsive. This was not a connection which she could see for herself and hers. Like her purchases, her life was to be the best she could find with what she had in her pocket.

[Undated]

"The blue flag is a relative of the troublesome hyacinth."

I find this note written on the back of a prescription for chemotherapy.

Why does this make me so sad? We are responsible for the nuisances committed by our relatives although perhaps we should not be.

Cancer is a relative of the most effective and necessary cells of our bodies.

For years I cherished my psychotic mother, gave her the best part of the house, for her honor which was her greatly needed medicine—Freud to the contrary notwithstanding. Meanwhile I walked with my eyes averted from my townsfolk, thinking that they thought of me only as her relative, and some of my dear friends would say, "You get more like your mother all the time." Not something to be ashamed of, since outside of her mental divergence, which was infrequent anyhow, she was a sweet and good person.

The troublesome hyacinth, I tell myself, is troublesome only north by northwest. It serves some purposes well.

Madness sometimes makes it possible to survive certain unbearable insults. It is a blue flag that grows then and is a relative to the trouble.

I am relative to madness but only so far. Blue, blue, my flag is certainly blue.

Sane or not sane, my mother is dead. And I may die soon of the troublesome cancer. We all die of something and it does seem very soon looking back on it. The hyacinth chokes the rivers and lakes, but it creates marshy conditions which serve an all important function in our ecosystem.

I am blue but willing. I look forward to ends and beginnings with flag held high, not as an end to trouble or being troublesome but as fertility of another kind, another kind of beginning.

THE MOST BEAUTIFUL GIRL IN THE WORLD

(for my mother)

With the hidden eyes of the baboon
Looking inside at her past
At the time when she was greatly honored
In a small town in Russia

The most beautiful girl in Russia
Made into a child-witch by the peasants
Because of her eerie beauty
Her eyes like the stormy sea

Which was a kind husband to her
In which she could swim and be loved
When she could no longer walk or stand
Looked at me puzzled and asked

"Where is my mama?" and had to be jolted
Back to her unpleasant painful present
Where this elderly homely woman
Was her daughter

THE NUT TREE

I had a little nut tree
Nothing would it bear
But a silver nutmeg
And a golden pear

A humming of song, subcutaneous
Surrounded me, a vapor of tunes like sweat
I was encased, unassailable nut
In the close-growing tree. Pages of the
Dictionary rose up like birds in the
Strong blue of the tropical sky, safe in
The dark glossy leaves of my little nut tree

> She banged her head against the wall, wailing
> Threw her feet up and down in a tantrum
> He covered her head with a coat
> For fear of the neighbors, listening
> And what could he do, after all, what else?
> It was the bottom line, the honor
> With which a man fills a woman
> He never heard of it
>
> She threw out the oriental carpets
> Lost her diamond rings
> Took the crystal chandeliers apart
> Used the Dresden platters for her sculpture
> Began to read about the suffragettes
>
> "Behemoth," he called her, angry, "Cow."
> She was silent, respectful
> Called out, choked, in the night
> Dreamt of dark intruders
>
> An almond, a cup and a knop
> Three daughters, three fates
> On this side three, on that side three
> Rose in the dictionary, encased in dreams
> Hands full of chandeliers, vases, degrees
> And the knot, the knout, ugly

TIME LASTS FOREVER

Behind her head lace curtains stirred
Behind her eyes light trembled, flashed
A storm brewed in her head
Shadows passed over her like birds

She sat as if in a wagon
Tasted danger the way blind children taste
To learn what surrounds them
No one was there. No one was coming

A small curl of a smile lit her face

She packed all her things every night
Like one who does not belong
Who must leave some night without warning
But this was not her plan. There was no plan

She allowed herself nothing
Nothing of yesterday
Less of tomorrow

The moment lasted and lasted
Time bloomed and flowered
Time lasted forever

HARD LINES

I carried my mother into the sea
for her joy in water.
It carried her easily, lovely water
her best daughter.

"Honor your mother and your father."
The word HONOR is not right.
In Hebrew it says, "Carry your mother
and father on your back." I did.

I carried my mother and father on my back.
And the Father of my fathers too.
They were heavy.
My back is strong. It needs a weight on it.

Cordelia and her sisters were different.
Cordelia had edges.
The sisters said there were no edges
between their father and themselves.

But from the other side of the hard lines
Cordelia was able to reach across and carry,
as was proper, as she was able.
The WORDS of the sisters carried Lear

Those words were his favorite daughters.

THE TASK

I carry a basket of small silver fish on my head
I must get it to the other side of the stream

There are round stones in the bed of the stream
I put my feet down one at a time slowly
If a stone shifts I move my foot to another

In the basket the fish move
They move like the stirrings of lust
Like a child in the fifth month they stir

My neck and head are balanced, tall under my burden
I do not look at the other side of the stream
I gaze beyond it or above it

I focus on an inner dimness patiently
A darkness far inside me
It gives quietness to the burden

Do not tip the silvery weight
Do not make it shift
Your tears make the stone slippery

Your fears make my feet unsure
Your loss prevents me
I must bring this breathing weight
To the other side of the stream

THE BEGINNING OF ANIMALS

He shone on the wall of the cave
unaware of me except as a kind of food
for his own use

He was larger and narrower than I
I could not understand what he was about
but I understood the peninsula of his body

It was unlike mine. He was warmer than I
and within me I felt cold
I had a need for heat around me

Inside me there was chaos.
I was empty, longing for order
He was a cave, a roof in bad weather

He was a comfortable place to sleep
from which I promised myself
I could get away whenever I wished

more alone and myself than I had been
He brought me down to the ground
to handle and study stones

not stones but the idea of them
ideas unnatural to me
rubbed my face raw on the earth

We lived together but apart
and I fed him with my part
of him absent in him

unless I was there outside
but when he was inside of me
I surrounded him and he learned

to dream, to be disconnected
from the wall, to float in
the beginning of animals

He learned to feed himself
on the picture of himself
on the wall of the cave

He did not grieve like me
He was hurt in his pride
and pushed, always pushed with his horns

We quarreled bitterly because
"I could not be him
He refused to allow me to be me"

although it was what kept his feet
alive and swift in the dirt.
We wore each other smooth by this

by filling and trying to match the difference
We were separate but we began to be alike
There developed a difficult resemblance

the way the leaves of past years
lie on the earth and begin to be earth
so we began to need

to fill each other less
because in any case we were already full
of the other one

surrounding and filling ourselves
each one and together
on the wall of the cave where we lived

NOT OF MY PEOPLE

I look into your face of water
Clear water, sunlit
I see groups of minnows
Embodied water, darting

With no plan. Planned.
No direction. Directed.

I see myself like mica
Like sand made from granite
Drifting down in your water
Catching your sunlight.

Who flows through you?
You perceive deeply to what
Conclusion? What fish
Will these minnows become

If they remain?
Who came before you?

Not mine. Mine.
Not made by me.
Made by me daily.

LOVE

The children and their mother
Go about
With prisms from a crystal chandelier
Held to their eyes

Theirs is a house of color
The stove is like a diamond

The father brings real diamonds
Satin-candy cushions
Crystal chandeliers

The mother pounds live fish
With a knife and mallet
Their scales shine like diamonds

The father gives his daughters coins
They shine them on his precious rugs

He brings them white furpieces
They sit and polish peachpits on a stone

He would bring them anything
He loves them so

HONEYMOON FOR FIVE ON THE ADRIATIC

Here is my mother in a cheap inn in Istria
75 cents a day for room and board
No running water pigs at the bottom of the latrines
In the blue Adriatic I lost my wide gold wedding band
Here we are kissing and kissing as usual
My mother was really young and beautiful then
We thought she was an old lady and snickered
When the Italian men followed her instead of us

Here is a Van Gogh bridge over the salt flats
Here we are all five taking a nap in the hot afternoon

This is around the corner from San Marco
We had given up our room on the Lido
And the Rhoda Bari our boat was not there
Mussolini may have made the trains run on time
But the sailors were off enjoying the fiesta
So we slept on the wire chairs outside of the cafe
Young country fellows in for the day
Guffawed at us and made remarks
I called them *caffoni* one of my few words
And they settled down respectfully
Agreeing with my choice of epithet

We were so thoroughly fucked out both of us
Although not beautiful, appealingly slavic and young
Our aura or smell attracted them like dogs

Here I am wearing two dresses the outer one wool
For warmth in the night outdoors
Here I am on my knees in the plaza San Marco
Not praying but feeding the pigeons their first handout
Here you are both the most beautiful men in Venice
Awakening on the steps of the church
Tall thin and young too. They must have thought you lovers
No one bothered you the fair and the dark

Here we are all five walking through narrow streets
We counted twenty seven cats in a small plaza
Some with bows of bedraggled ribbon
Everyone fed them but they remained scrawny
From making love constantly

Here in a narrow alley is the procuress
She looked like a housewife and probably was
She tried several tongues finally German
"Kommen sie mit?" and Lou said, "Was verkaufen sie denn."
"Madchen" She said impatiently, "Schone junge madchen"
And you both turned away
That was thoroughly taken care of
We had a neverending hankering

LETTER TO A SOLDIER 1943

You do so little gushing
Your letters might be read by anyone
But what you say is so condensed
Carries such a punch
It is only for the one person

These long-married men about to go into the army
Have a sort of inward look a hush a stocktaking
A gathering of long unused forces
It is their first day of school again
One would wish to strengthen them
But they are on their own

I was disturbed and ashamed by her fault
I asked whether I could ask a frank question
It was too shaming and I did not ask
All the time that uncomfortable stare
Away from my eyes and me
Her attention always returning
To my birth certificate on the desk
Father's birthplace Volkovisk
Father's occupation rabbi
Religion Jewish
There was no possible opening she said
I had done too well on the tests

If something has been wrong
We must set about working with what is left
If nothing is wrong we must prove it to each other
There would be an end to reticence on painful subjects

YOUNG GIRL

The armory is dark
built of thick stone
It has no windows
but dimly from inside
I hear a band
and marching feet.

The gull shrieks
and drops
to scissor a sick fish
twisting like a heart.

The mallard lies limp
in a butcher shop.
It has lead pellets inside
and a bloody neck
where a dark blue rainbow gleams.

The small river is full,
It tears between its banks
and rolls big rocks against each other.

The tree hides
a cosmopolis of sparrows
making arrangements.
The leaves tremble.

ARIES THE RAM

We were together for the first time
Like a summer storm far away
Far lightning, separate from the others.
You were not listening to the music.
You were pounding home the points,
Pointing out wrongs and thundering.

You blew ash, hot stones, poured lava
Got red as ochre under the eyes
Insisted on clear thinking, on justice
Angry. You were angry.
Anyone could lose face who got in your way.
You were a steel hammer hot with beating wood
A trumpet, brassy, full of clangor, metallic.

I found you could be quietened
Your throat smelled like sweet grass
Like hay (like myrrh, as they say)
Your eyes, the familial rubies
Ox-eyes, dropping at the corners
Sad and feverish
The taste of your new mouth, basil fresh
The two of us welling up hot and winy
Virgin except for each other.

I had never known what a man's body was
Had no brothers, my father full of decorum
The surprising man-changes, like a phoenix
Rising from the fire all new.
Over and over the rooster, the woodpecker
Vermillion-capped and the strange smell

Of pepper or broth, garlicky, hot as mustard
Drawing me down in spite of my raising
The hair-silky thighs
Of the Arabian gazelle, the saluki
The strokable jaguar, the nettle
That sings and causes the blood to ooze.

And here, now, after a lifetime of years
We pull toward each other and hold
That fleshy magnet still new.
We strike still like flint on stone.
My cedar tree, my garland of acanthus
Covered with spiny teeth and hurting
Holding my hand quietly, so quietly, all night.

LONGING FOR THE BIG UMBRELLA

Longing for the sheltering wing of the big umbrella
has made you thin.
Longing for the horse-hair fly whisk
has made you ill.
You walk high and insulted
like a camel.
Come out from under the bed.
Here are many-colored flies like stars
which do not sting.
Here is an umbrella under which you are chief.

ALTHO THE WREN

Altho the wren
whispers songs
to her nestlings
and the cat simmers
pleasant
under a covering of kittens
I hum in a thin voice
to my
sister's new son
and try to do well

BUOY

It's because of the yearning of cats in her head
The swallows in the barn of her eyes
The smell as of roses or health
Above the weeping of wounds

It is because of the squeaking of counterfeit hearts
The teeth of ice smiling, immune
The howling of dogs at the take-cover siren
The tired flies buzzing the glass

It is because though she's here she's not here at all
That she rocks on the waves and she chimes
When the wind or the waves bend her all the way over
The weight of her past sets her right

74

TOUCHED, I OOZE

Touched I ooze
Sticky I dry rubbery
A nuisance, exposed to air
Coagulate

As sowthistle, Brimstone-wart
Sunspurge, North American asclepius
Videlicet milkweed

When cracked or broken
I bleed white
Stick to the fingers
Blacken them like tar
Shrink, wrinkle, decline

Oh, to be like the others
Flexible, pruned, apart in space
Restrained
Not so lavish with my milky ectoplasm

WE SMILE, WE WOMEN

Ho, the hollows he will fill
With his little dibber
His chick-pea, his acorn

He pisses in a long yellow arc
In his own face
Is startled and cries

His large head bobbles
It warms the space
Where my neck meets my shoulder
He climbs my left breast
And belches, then yawns

HOMEMAKING CLASS

Of all my brothers and sisters, he said,
I am the only one who does not know his father.
        Do you have different fathers?
We have three, he said, but mine makes four.
I never knew him.
        You are your father, I said
        and theirs too
        since you are the oldest,
        and look in the mirror, come—
        do you see a father?
Yes, he said, I will be a good father,
        And we went on counting plates:
        Four cracked. Set them aside.
        Twenty three bread and butters.
        Now spoons.
        Pile them in a stack. Sixteen.
But they go to visit their father sometimes, he said.
        You are a very good person, I said, You can be counted on.
Yes, he said, and went on counting.

WELCOMING OLD FRIENDS

Ho
Break.the pots
Throw out the stove
See who has come to my door!
We are like the two feet of the compass
Pointed and apart but
Circling each other

October 27, 1979

Shabbos. That special quiet, joy with a hint, just a little, of tedium. A brisk, cold day, sunny, no work. We went to *shul,* which I love, the accustomed prayers, the Hebrew letters and words, sweet as my mother's lap and rocking chair, and the occasional brightening of the text, a sharpened vision as if all were being read through a burning glass, so that the letters leave the paper a little and are darker, separate. Then I feel a kind of breathlessness, a waiting for something, but not at all incomplete, the contrary, a longed for perfection. The passages where this happens have no particularity. I can never find out why or when this occurs. Sometimes it does not happen for a long while. I would say that it depends on how well I pray, but often it comes when I seem not to be praying with any special concentration. The light in the *shul* is awful. It actually interferes with the reading, but when I see this way it is as if the book provided its own light. So many of the prayers are about light. *Ehl adon* is particularly lovely. "The lights which HE had made are lovely." Except that the Hebrew words and the tunes that go with them are their own, solitary transfiguration. The words I use are vulgar. They diminish the joy.

January 19, 1980

Went to synagogue. I follow the services with accustomed ease, finally. Something is lost in the ability to follow, the loss of the effort, of clambering on glass walls to follow and comprehend the Hebrew. The habitual devotions are read at breakneck speed. They must be. As it is, services start at 8:20 and do not finish until twelve. If a pace which allows for some true devotion were used, the morning prayers would take all day, then where would there be time for afternoon and evening prayers, not to mention eating and resting and other Sabbath pleasures? Sometimes I do not try to keep pace but focus on certain small prayers, another one each time, trying to get what I can in depth out of that one, rather than get a little from each breathless task.

A task it has been. For years, Jacob and I have been doing what can almost not be done, wandering lost after these virtuosi of prayer, the true and mostly, bored, afficionados of the complete service, seven days a week, three times a day. The reason, I imagine that *Hashem* prefers *t'shuvah,* repentance, is that the penitent (or as it is in Hebrew, the turner-around) experiences each prayer, each word, in fact each letter, with the intensity of something unaccustomed, difficult and amazing.

81

Somewhat, I have lost that first intensity along with the feeling of bewildering effort. Sometimes a passage will glow up new and sharp, jump out of the run of loaded, time-filling custom. Even so there is a good, calm feeling of accomplishment, even on the least inspired Saturday. Inspired! Breath, full of breath. When a passage is strongly felt I perceive a change in my breathing. I breathe more shallowly and much less. Almost I do not breathe at all. When I used to come to the unwanted and premature ending of one of my pregnancies, after a number of such occurrences, I learned how, by slow, deep breathing, I could help the inevitable, if miserable, process along so that it did not last too long or cause too much physical discomfort. Breathing, too, is related to the orgasm. Incorrect breathing can impede its oncoming. In certain societies where the focus is on these natural accomplishments it may be that instruction in breath-control is part of the secret learning of adolescents, their coming-of-age instruction. There are these separate houses for men and women in the so-called savage societies. Such a simple, natural thing, to breathe. Yet there are many kinds. Maybe cowardice itself may be due to incorrect breathing in dangerous situations — and bravery a sort of fortunate discovery certain people make for themselves.

April 21, 1980

I have been reading Edmond Jabes in Rosmarie Waldrop's translation. After the poems there is a comment and critique by Maurice Blanchot, translated by Waldrop and Paul Auster. There is an essay on *Interruption* since Jabes' work interrupts itself, so to speak. Silence is his method. By making interruptions he creates silences. This is the "leap" of poetry. Jabes uses the question of being Jewish — the fate of the Jews makes being Jewish a question — for the grief which is uppermost in his poems. He equates the writer with the Jew, in the sense, I suppose, that the writer is not of the people, the ordinary. Blanchot refers, in a note to his commentary on *The Book of Questions* to the book *Difficile Liberté* (edition Albin Michel)—in which "Emmanuel Levinas, with his customary depth of authority in speaking of Judaism speaks of what concerns us all, I find, among many essential reflections, the following: 'The oral law is eternally contemporaneous to the written . . .'" When I see Levinas' name and read the accustomed truths I experience a breathlessness, a sort of attentiveness which prayer and my religion bring me. The poem I wrote *Deus Absconditus* (retitled *We Love Him Absent*) was based on a piece of Emmanuel Levinas', which he had drawn from the writings of someone who was killed in the death-camps, a very religious and pure Jew, Mordecai, I think, who wrote to God, remonstrating with Him. Levinas took off from there. We all, we Jews, take off from each other.

May 9, 1980

I have just read an answer to Said's book by my cousin Hillel Halkin in the Commentary magazine. Hillel is a very able writer, a capable intellect. Things are painful for those Jews who live in Israel. Are they to be forced by the opinion of all the world, even many Jews, to a settlement of the Palestinian question which will destroy them as a country? They dig their heels in and, properly, refuse to preside over their own destruction. It is for this time that they were made a stiff-necked people. I felt much more a whole person there, where others took for granted exactly what I did—that we must survive and survival requires that we think ahead and refuse solutions which are new problems, worse than the old ones. To be confronted by people who are well-loved friends, who come to harmful conclusions for small prizes in their careers (really) is very painful. I keep off such subjects for reasons of friendship. This is as much a dirty compromise as what they are doing.

AS I AM MY FATHER'S

I am my own
My opinions and feelings
Are my own

I do not conceal
Or deny what I am
What you put there

In the end
At the end of days
You will be just

Like Balaam
Who beat his ass
For seeing

What was there
You beat us
These many times

But in the end
You will see the angel too
Since you put this angel

In our way
You will be just
Since justice is your name

I do not speak of mercy
Which is your name too

THE WIVES OF HILLEL AND ISAIAH

The dark fire, the blue-black fire
Of His distillation
Around them
Has not consumed them

The fire burns them. They are not consumed
The dark blue fire for which they are the fuel
Is surrounded by a bright fire, a yellow fire

Radiance is above it, around it
Not fire but effulgence
The fire burns them. They are not consumed

As holy as pure as the substance of the heavens
Past, present and future are one to them
In its light they plainly remember

What happened in the future
This radiance of easy commitment
Fueled by the faith of the wives

Of Hillel and Isaiah, a dark light
A dark faith, blue-black burning
Like a clean, straight wick in a candle

Burning their physical being, they are links
In a chain that draws down His power
Incomprehensible

Essential around their men. The wives
Of Hillel and Isaiah, the fire burns them
They are not consumed

WE LOVE HIM, ABSENT

(After Emanuel Levinas)

Direct contact with the sacred without daily service
is madness. What demon, what strange magician
populates our heaven now that it is a desert?

Who seeks to be a saint, to be like God
in a place where He has proved Himself not to be?
Any grandmother, any gardener can prove the certainty

of His existence daily under an empty sky.
Atheism is legitimate. Monotheism braces, supports it.
There is no bed, no pillow, no bosom, on which

to fall asleep in tears, so take over that role.
For the gardener, worms and beetles can not
expiate their sins; he is not a mystic.

The grandmother gathers together her small flock
of the just, abandoned to their own justice.
She happily feeds them her good cooking.

She scrubs away suffering sent by a veiled and
distant God. She renounces all beneficial manifestations.
God does not triumph except as tidiness.

That is her conscience, to bring order from chaos.
She is Jewish because that is what she insists on being
a daily follower of order. The suffering of the just for

justice makes her Jewish. God does not love her.
She loves God. There is no tenderness here.
They are not equals. There is no sentimentality.

There is no communion. There is Torah.
Torah is not absent. It is not veiled.
She does His order because she must.

Order is what He should stand for. She loves it
better than she loves Him. He being absent.
Who has not been destroyed in His name among us?

He owes us! We have debts also. She is not resigned.
Why should she be? He can not run away from us
nor can He make us stop loving Him, absent.

Is our adoration burdensome to Him?
He has removed His face. There is no need.
We are not equals. We are exalted by our persistence.
We are full of exaltation.

CLOTHE WHAT IS LEFT

First soak a long time in water
Clean the body well
Especially wash away anger
The feeling of having been wronged
Anger prevents joy from passing
Inward and outward

Let green-growing branches
Form from your fingers and eyes
Sing like a beech tree
In a pleasant, rainy voice
Allow your vegetable self to rejoice

Then comfort your animal self
Wash the fur of your sex with
Your tongue. Smooth the fur
Behind your ears, over your belly
Eat good meat. Drink fine wines

Now turn your thoughts
To what is near
How the sky is blue
How water is wet
Do not strain after hard thoughts
Let yourself study sayings
You have known since childhood

Then gaze, unfocused, at the letters
The words of what *they* have written
The incomprehensible, the impenetrable
Thoughts written in forgotten tongues

What you cannot take in
What is too hard for you
Detaches your self from your senses

Move lightly now, without effort
Skipping and skimming
The motion awakens the memory
Until these thoughts come back to you
Out of the past, orderly, easy to take in

Now pass beyond your animal being
Your vegetable thoughts, beyond
Thoughts, words, bread, wind, earth
Draw yourself out of your pocket
Like a small round mirror
A whirling circle of bright light
Finally all light, all form, all spirit
Left behind, what is left
Must be clothed
Clothe it

THE LETTERS OF THE BOOK

Aleph the cow with wide horns
Her milk in the night sky
Walks slowly on clouds
Aleph to the tenth power
She leads with symbolic logic
To the throne of milky pearl
Aleph the sky-cow with lovely eyes
Wide-horned giver she gives mankind
Her sign of is-ness. The cow

Bayz the house   snug
Under the heat of the sun
Out of the rain and the snow
We curl up in a corner
Under the roof of Bayz
Out of the daily sorrow
Bayz the comforter
Inhabited by humanity
Cat-like and childlike
Inside of his Bayz

Ghimel the camel
Carries man into the book
The leaves and waves
Of the forest the sea of the book
Boat of the desert the camel
Long traveler drinking the task
Ghimel drinks the dry road of daily observance
It slakes the thirst for communion

Daled the door like a wall
No hinges no handle
Daled the mysterious opener
Into a place with a road
The six hundred and thirteen small roads
Of derekh eretz

Mem is the water
Sweetly obeying
The red-raging water
Which parted
Mem came together
And drowned the pursuers
Stubborn refusers of freedom
The enslavers Mem drowned them
Mem was the water
Brackish tormenting
Sweetened with leaves
By our Moses
The waters of trust
Which he struck from the rock
Mem mayim water

The jelly-glowing eye full of love
Sees past the eye the Ayin
Like a dog it perceives the hidden
It turns and stares at its master
It pleads with him to come home
The longing for certainty
Fills him too full
Return, my master, he says
Your eye to my eye
Ayin

Peh the mouth speaking hastily
Praying easily fast without reverence
Full of gossip causing estrangement
Let my soul be as dust to Peh
The loud quarreler the prattler
The carrier of tales to and fro
The beguiler the mouth Peh better still

I have swallowed Vav the hook
It had something tasty and nourishing on it
A promise of plenty and friendship
With someone more than myself
I've got Vav the hook in my gut
I shift to rearrange the discomfort

Like a sharp minnow inside
When he draws up the line
Attached to the hook
When he rips the Vav out
There will be strange air around me
Burning my gills

Yod the hand
And Koff the palm
Rested gently
On Raish the head
Of Abraham our father
Who crossed over
Burning the idols
Behind him in Ur
He looked upward
At stars sun and moon
Then looked further
For a pat on the head
From Yod and Koff
The unseen hand and palm

In the crook
Of the Lammed leaning forward
I put my neck when I pray
My shepherd makes me meek
He makes my knees bend
He guides me I follow
With the loop of the Lammed
On my throat
I go

Shin is the tooth
It chews on the word
(With the dot on the left
It is Sin)
So much sharper than Shin the tooth
Is learning in the study
Together by dimlight
Chuckling together at the tooth
The horn that was known to gore
The tooth for a tooth in our story
The sharp-toothed father
Of our fathers
Who was wont to gore in the past

LETTER WRITTEN IN THE YEAR OF THE CARRYING AWAY TO BABYLON

My Kinsman Hanamel,

The deed is buried by the Horse Gate
On the side of Jerusalem looking inward
Toward the place of gifts and sacrifices

Tell your children born away from home
To write the place on their hearts
Let them set their teeth into the carrying away
Let them bite the hurt places hard

Remember where the deed is
Remember where the field is

Let them be mild and untroublesome there
So they may not be diminished
In times of evil let them be silent and discreet
So they may save a remnant to return

My near kinsman Hanamel, my uncle Shallum's son
I was commanded to buy your field
The voice was familiar and so was the time
I pay you these seventeen shekels of silver
Weighed and witnessed by reliable men

So that after the Chaldeans have gone
After their fruit has withered from above
After their root has dried from below
Those of ours that remain may return

> In dreams my faith is not painful
> Someone burns my mouth with coal
> And it does not hurt me to believe
> It does not hurt to speak dreamspeech

Beastseed and manseed increase in your
well watered field

> Jeremiah, your uncle's son

TO BE REMEMBERED

There are walls there
Beneath other walls
And others beneath them

There are cities there
From earliest time
From before there was writing

They were built of fired brick
From bitumin, a sort of black slime
Used for mortar

The city Birs Nemroud
Is too large to be believed
It is a natural phenomenon
Said the experts

No man had a hand in it
It is now exactly as it was
When Alexander saw it, they say

The tower of Belus
Was destroyed by fire
By a meteor or lightning bolt
Millennia ago

They said to one another
Come let us make bricks
Bricks for stone
Bitumin for mortar
We will build us a city
A tower
We will make us a name
To be remembered

Nebuchadnezzar
Caused to be written
By a scribe
On clay tablets
What he did for Imgur-Bel

To make the city of Babylon
Into a fortress a bulwark
A wall so thick
With earthen embankments
Quays of burnt brick
Against the wall within
A moat like a flood
Like the sea, doors of cedar
Overlaid with copper

Where now is
Nebuchadnezzar?
And where is the wall
East of Babylon?

The tablets remain
To be remembered

THE CHOICE

The idea of coming through
Of continuing as a
Hand in hand pair
With a creature, not a creature
A face with no face

The idea of not questioning
Of obeying the impossible
Of promises not questioned
(Not laughing at them)

Of what should be
Without miracle or promise
A surfeit, a day by day
Acceptance and even refusal

The friendship of an old horse
With the burden that breaks it
In the face of reason
A thirst for water

From the well guarded by enemies
A taste of honey from the hive
Built in the carcass
Of a lion

The cat who persists
In having kittens in the
Culvert, time after time
A land promised

Already inhabited by giants
Hidden meanings too difficult
Seized on, held onto
In love without reason

The choice of the chosen
To love daily
To obey in spite of unreason
Chosen for that only

To persist beyond reason
To take survival as the gift
A sign of trust in the choice
Unlearning the past

The repetition of the past
In the present
The repetition of the past
In the future

Eyes shut tight to the
Impossibility of the promise
Walking through stone walls
For a cup of water from a well guarded by enemies

COLLAGE

The artist is glued to his drawing board
He is cutting up old drawings
And collaging them. He can't stop
Making new shapes with jokes in them

There is a slight ennui in the work however
Since the art of the virtuoso is like "God
Paring his fingernails" while spinning off
New worlds.
               Lately chassidim have moved
Into our town. They wear fur hats even in
Summer and layers of black clothing.
They walk down our street to their
Constant prayers, their eyes on the ground.
No one, nothing, penetrates their many
Layers of thoughts, dreams, black cloth.
They are closed in their own
Intentional strangeness.
                  Because of the
Tay-Sachs babies and the no-babies
And the children who are friendly
Only with machines, our people are beginning
To mate by splicing their inbred shoots
Into wilder stock. Like rare apples or roses
Before their particularity puts an end to them

And the nations will sigh with relief
"Look," they'll say, "they're gone.
No gas chambers, no soap factories.
They did it themselves. All we had to do
Was wait a while and let them do it."

And the new kinds, the sweet yellow apples
The five-color roses, grown on hardier stock
Will they turn again?
                          And how will it be
When they do not suck an aleph dipped in
Honey, when the first page of the hard book
Is no longer smeared with honey to be licked
By the youngest scholars
                               when the hand that
Cups the small buttocks no longer holds
The book as well? And our mother Sarah
No longer whispers, *"Rabbenu shel olam."*
Our teacher of the world, as she
Kisses the downy head on the fontanelles
Open and soft to Him? O Him. He
Rabbenu shel olam is bored with us
He pares his nails and may choose
The Chinese or Indians who are easier
To deal with and more enthusiastic
About multiplication, the first
Of the six hundred and thirteen
Difficult requirements.

THE SMOKE BY DAY

Put us up in little bottles
Make pills of the air from our lungs
Feed eighteen drops to the heads
Stoned on our benedictions

Debauch the cardinals, beguile the meuzzins
With smoke from the furnace that burns us
Let the Russians and Prussians
Breathe the sweat of our finish

The air will be drunken, visionary
The light shaken, prophetic
The waters contagious with Hosannas
Halleluiah forever.

IN LOVE

When we were first in love
When we were young
You held me
By the back of my neck
With your fingers and your thumb
We walked along that way

It made my knees go soft
It made me
Meek
I bowed where you bent me

> In the prayer book
> There is a *lammed*
> It is a shepherd's crook
> It leans forward to
> Grab me

> I put my neck in there
> In the crook
> Of the *lammed* leaning forward

> When I say my prayers
> I put my head
> In the crook
> It grabs me

> My shepherd makes me
> Meek
> He makes my knees bend

> Lead me
> I follow
> Guide me. Send me
> With the loop in the *lammed*
> I go
> I bow where you bend me

THE BRINGER

He was hungry
There was no food
The land was dry
They hunted him
He hid and fasted

When the wind blew
When it thundered
When the sky cracked
He could not hear it

When he sat quiet
He was still
He breathed quietness
He heard it

He poured water
He wet the wood
He asked it to be a fire
It was a fire

He will come back soon
Will come to my family
He will bring Someone
We keep the door open

We keep a room for him
For when he comes, a small room

THE PROPHET

The prophet works hard at dreaming
He allows his dreams to take over

He was not born a prophet
He was born able to become one

As the lammergeyer comes out of its egg
Bald and weak but with soaring

Coded in its cells for the future
Able to learn to seek far below it

The gift of prophecy comes out in sad times
To the proper one who has prepared himself

By persistent practice to be able
To be strongwinged and wise for soaring

To follow the prediction of his dreams
Far down on the ground where his kin

Lie helpless and dying of cold
Like lambs to the lamb-vulture in spring

THE WITNESS

Not a prophet, he says of himself
But a witness, like Nicodemus
Standing foursquare, close to the ground
Reaches his arm way out and points
To what was there all the time

The young men crowd around
For a taste of the crumbs
From his full mouth. They listen
They repeat. *"Agapae," he said, "not Eros."*
Explaining what was there plainly

His square grey beard, his rooted feet
His open eyes, looking through
Looking right into them
Their wavering meaning, meeting it
Plain as a board, to themselves now too

Making straight to the spiral
Thinking of the theologists
The historians full of praise
Praise unwelcome to him, he says
Simple, breathing loud like a

Small horse delighted to be
Trotting on grass, breathing fresh air
He is "freed from the belief
That there is no freedom
Therefore he is free."

ZIPPORA RETURNS TO MOSES AT REPHIDIM

By the wells
Alone and running
You found my dark skin a comfort
A home of maternal wetness

Now I bow, since I must
To your unseen Lover

My son is well named a stranger
For me

If there are others
You may cut them
Before they have learned to suck
Using bronze not stone
Oh bitter husband to me

Distracted lover
I shall sleep in your tent alone

My father has brought me back
He will stay to teach you
To govern your inconstant people
Constant only in revolt

It was his craft brought you this far
His and the hand of your Bridegroom

No more shall I be troubled
By the smiles of my six glutted sisters

Send your Nubian concubine to me
We shall both be darkly forsaken
While you fast
And adore in the wind
Your jealous
Bridegroom of blood

WELCOMING SISERA

He asked for water. I gave him milk.
Sleep! Child of my milk and couch.
Bronze sword crusted with blood
Unsheathed on the floor
Fingers and feet dreaming
Motions of battle.

The pin of the tent
And the mallet strong in my hand
In! Warm at his temple like milk.
His mother waits.

ISAAC AND ESAU

Who comes to us in our dark
Smelling of innocence?

The tent being full of dream sheep
We need no increase of real flocks.

Is there a dream we can give the child
Plain as hunger?

We hear him weeping, helpless
Against eyes that cut through sky

For the customary ram
Familiar to our darkness

THE ORDER

There was hyssop in bunches
and scarlet wherever you looked
but we never could follow instructions

Fire. We should have used fire
as we were advised and
waited twice seven days

The mattresses took sick in there
It did no good to cart them away
time after time

We killed one of the birds
mixed its blood with water
scoured and sprinkled

but the stones
even the stones
had veins of green rot

It was starting out wrong
and the small changes
in the order of cleansing
prevented a cure
In fact we still haven't
set the second bird free

MORE RAYS

He readied himself
He stayed awake to be ready
He washed. He changed his clothes.
As it was ordered he did it.
He washed again.
Seven times he washed and changed.
Went in and out, moved from here to there

His face shone
Like the evening sun on the brass shovels
Like the sun on the water
Like the heart of the sun itself

More rays
More rays how can
More rays than can

He followed the special order of touching
He washed and changed

To think of it makes us sad
Now we are nothing
We cannot see his clothes
We can never see his face
His ordered motions
From wall to curtain
In and out
We cannot see that wall
Those curtains, that time.

ACCORDING TO THE ART OF THE APOTHECARY

Stacte, galbanum, onycha
spices with frankincense
of each an equal weight
a perfume a confection
>Thin, beat it, well
>Small, small, talk to it
>The voice is good for the tempering
According to the days around the sun
so many manehs
and three over by handful
for atonement

Balm, onycha, galbanum and frankincense
seventy manehs
Myrrh, cassia, spikenard, saffron
sixteen manehs
Costus, twelve
>Make pleasant the offering
>as in days of old
>as in ancient years.
The rind of an odoriferous tree
three
cinnamon, nine
soap of Carsina
nine kabs
wine of Cyprus (or capers)
three seahs and three kabs
and if Cyprus wine could not be found
a strong white wine

Salt of Sodom
one quarter kab
Ma'aleh'ashan, a herb, a pinch
amber of Jordan, a little
Honey makes it profane.
If honey were added
no man could stand
because of the odor.
If prepared with any omission
one incurs the penalty of death

The balm from an incision in
the trunk of the balsam tree
Why soap of Carsina?
To refine the onycha or cloves
to make it handsome
Why wine of Cyprus?
To harden the cloves by soaking.

To prepare a half is right
but a quarter or a third
we have not heard it to be right.
  Thin, thin, beat it small.
  Talk to it
  The voice is good for the tempering.
  Surround me with songs.
  Be a hiding place to me.
  Answer in the day when we call.

THE COUNTING MADE THE CORNERS RIGHT

The counting made
The corners
Of the building
True

One
One and one
Two
Two and one

Four horns
Corners
One and seven he counted
One and six

The goat stayed fluid
It steamed
Yellow eyes, square pupils
Fringes of flesh at its throat

They beat him with sticks
They threw stones at him
They sent him away
The goats were a gift
Both goats
One to die and one to drive away

One
One and one
Two
Two and one

The counting was washing
It was clean
It was for the building

NORTH

The north on the north
The holiest side of the altar
Northward the side for the bull and the goat
The he-goat killed for atonement
Their blood received in a vessel
On the north

Blood sprinkled between the staves of the ark
Before the veil of the golden altar
Northward

The offering for the people
For each person
The sin-offering at the north

The he-goat for new-moons, for festivals
At the north

The burnt offering for robbery
For taking sacred object
For breaking in on a betrothed handmaiden
For rape the offering burnt, sacrificed
On the north

Oh snow and wind obeying His voice
Mountain high on the side of the north
Snow like wool
Frost like ashes
Morsels of ice

The blast of His nostrils breaks the windows of the sky
He sends hail, snow, vapours, stormy winds obeying His word

HAPPY THE EYE THAT SAW US

Happy the eye that saw us
As the raiment worn by the patriarchs
As a garden of jewels in his crown
Fearful as pure nitre

To the others as a light in a forest
As the purling of bells in his skirts
When we were the true corner of the house
When we shone with the light of testimony

Happy the eye that beheld us
At one under the curtains of heaven

Like lightning from the face of the angel
A warning of blue fringe in the corner of nations
We shared a particular awareness
We glowed in a rainbow of witness

THE SLAUGHTERER

The ivory handled knife is square in his hand
It feels at home
He keeps a bluestone in his closet
In a velvet case with the footlong knife
The whetting of it is his art

Stands deep in blood in rubber boots
On a concrete floor gridded for drainage
Smiles at children
Is not bloodthirsty

The slaughterer is necessary
Bears no ill will
Sees the elegance of the animal for its purpose

He laughs at stunting years spent hungry
His trade has kept him full
The days ate him. He eats them.

He laughs as if lizards crawled on him
Half a shudder

THE FIFTIETH YEAR

Like self-heal
They had grown in waste places
Clearings, along roadsides

Their healing properties
Not borne out by modern science
But here they were
After fifty such years

       Butter-blond boys from Austria in *lederhosen*
       Holy men from Morocco in coats of many colors
       Ethiopians in time-worn blue-serge suits
       Beneath, around and hanging out of
       The eucalyptus trees
       They had come here finally
       From far parts of our eggshaped planet

       All pierced by the same thorns
       Looking deep into each other's eyes
       Each under the banner of his own
       Segment of the family
       The lion, the deer, the ass, the ship
       And so forth

       There were thirty chanters
       Each as different
       As we were from each other
       They were chanting a song
       The same song thirty times
       Every time touching his own kin
       And us all

       The Falasha from Ethiopia was humming
       Along with the chanter of his people
       He was trembling
       Tears were running down his dark cheeks
       They were wetting his kinky earlocks
       He was swaying the way my grandfather had swayed
       There was a reddish light coming out of his tears
       Like soft red raspberries, like bee-balm

The fiftieth year would hardly come again
For anybody here
Nor had any of us been in this place
The fiftieth year before this one
We were here for each other
To be strong together
To prevent bad dreams
We took the coming together
Like self-heal
To cure the trembling

ATHENS AND JERUSALEM

I

Tipping down from above the clouds at Athens
we saw the roots of the islands growing out
of the old Greek soil. The sea in separate
layers of frothy white, winedark and pale
cerulean blue around the immodest roots
of the old-tooth islands. The air here was
good as in Jerusalem, dry smelling of
grey rosemary and thyme, but it did not tremble.
The gold light was quiet and calmly still.
The girls were Greek, from Greece a long time and dressed
reasonably in the reasonable, measured
light of the old, culpable gods. "No one is
coming. We are here. We wear plain woolens to
keep warm as we did two thousand years ago.
We are not waiting for anyone. They were here.
But it is not that important. We are here
in the light and the dry, clear air of our past,
of our daily past and our daily future."

II

Well, if the waters rise up
to the east and the west here
on this street where the bus runs
and the gaudy copies of
Persian rugs hang over the balconies to sun and where
the pudding-breasted houris
from Marrakesh lean over
the window sills, Jews, what will
the Messiah look like on
that Day? Here in the light that
is much more than light, in the
singing sweetness of golden
motes, in the honeyed breath of
the Shechina, the Messiah

will wear an Italian silk
suit cut in the latest mode
and drive a fine, white sports car.
Its roar and take-off will bring
all the curly wives out of
the recesses of their
one room flats to lean their full
breasts on the sills with garish
machine made pillows to OH
at the Man as beautiful
as the latest movie star
in a white car the like of
which has not until this Day
been seen in Jerusalem

KIBBUTZ

The air is dry and smells healing.
The night is quiet.
There is a whiteness through the dark.
Here the beaten and chastened meat of young Jews
swells and pounds with blood.
The night is rest.
The children call like sirens,
Sweet birds call, "abba, abba."

The young men stand in a circle.
They toss a boy child from hand to hand.
The heavy wives,
Their eyes deep waters of giving,
go slowly home,
one by the hand and one in the belly.
The fathers laugh and frighten the boy babies
into calm warriors.

A sparrow is dying in the dry dust behind the kitchen,
Where greasy cans rust.
I fill a can with water
and hold the tiny no-bones in my hand
to make it drink.
I only speed the dry death with terror.

THE CHILDLESS WOMAN, THE AKIRA

The childless mother of children
Tilts like a gull on the air
She sails supported by nothing

The children of the akira
The childless mother of children
Steal the air from under her wings

They lie in a pit and dream dreams
They sit by the side of the pit
And interpret the dreams of the dreamers

They love death and the wasting of seed
Children are a nuisance to her daughters
They turn to each other for joy

The sons of the childless mother
Take the air from under her breast
They curse her. They join the others that hurt her

The sons of the Akira, the childless woman
Cut off their seed. They look in the mirror with hatred
She sails like a gull on nothing

PRESENCE

Citron
Fruit of light
Odor of brightness
Singing and branching
Seed of adoration
Bowing again to the
Corners and points
Of the homeland of light

Here is the City
The City is here
Here is the River
The River flows by

Melting the knots
Of seeing, of hearing
Into a fragrance
Of Citron of Myrtle

That Stream hid
A glinting, a darting
With its eye on the City
Sometimes he spoke to it near

By the border of dream
On the edge of feeling
In a split in a rock
Where sound was not

Nor light nor scent
He felt the presence
Of a Sound unheard
Of a flowering Light
That could not be seen

That other self
That only awoke
When the focus was poor
That depended for its blooming
On the sleep of attention
Loosened, untied
And opened a door
To let through a trace
Of a Presence white hot
Rushing through space.
Scattering clouds, disks
Spheres of being

IN THE TABERNACLE OF RUSHES

Down   Bow   Rustle   Sway
Point straight up. Bow Rustle
Point over left shoulder   Bow   Rustle
Point over right shoulder Bow Rustle

Sight out Hear myrtle   Rustle
Smell light Citron
Taste air   Bow
Touch woven leaves   Sway

Grasp   Bow   Rustle   Sway
Forwards Sideways   Sideways   Up
Eyes shut see darkness
Eyes half-open see darkness
Eyes open see darkness
Smell light Citron
Clear the eyes Drink the water alive
Put out the smoke with the fire
Smell it beginning

UNDER THE SHAWL

The great beasts rumble and sway.
It is dark down here under my father's shawl,
Sweet and familiar behind his knee.
I play with the fringe and look up into
The forest of nostrils and beards.

A careful power lifts my child-bones up
To the lectern where the smell of snuff
And the peppery man-smell, the great rough hands
And the coarse grandpa clothes comfort me.

The place smells the same as once
And drones too as I remember.
My bones feel small. I am lifted easily.

THE DARK SCENT OF PRAYER

In the tunnel
Light is haloed
Sound dissolved
The skin of separation
Is softened

Thought approaches
Airy and bright
Soft but pervasive
It penetrates rock

Where no edges are tight
The despairing hornet
Can fly through
Stained glass

Frightened sparrows
Can soar through clouds
Painted on the ceiling

The striped wasp
Confused by the Book
Can thrive on
The dark scent of prayer

YOU

Down below
the dog whimpers and sighs.
It is I.
Outside
a boat lows.
It is I.

Was it the rain in its seasons I heard?
Or am I weeping?
My teeth chatter as with cold.
Where is the good land
that you promised me?

You kick the wheel
and put your strange hands on the clay.
I turn.
You find and draw up.
I breathe. I tremble.
Oh Lord!
Here am I.

IV

December 1, 1979

In my backyard are two spruces, not blue, just regular green spruces. They are a male and a female tree, a pair. The male is thicker branched with more needles but no pinecones. The female has many russet cones. They start out green then turn orange, russet, brown. Then they fall to the ground where the squirrels gnaw them away to the center stem of each cone. The male tree is full of birds. They nest in the upper branches. The squirrels too seem to have a summer nest up near the top of the male tree. The birds and squirrels like to sit on the branches of the female tree and look about. It is much more open and gives a better view of the yards around the tree. Bluejays will warn of a prowling cat from the more open tree. I am told that in nature that is the function of a bluejay, to be a warner. The other birds rely on its cry, a raucous sort of bronx cheer, not too different from the sound of a crow.

April 23, 1980

I went to visit M., to ask her to start the herb seeds I had purchased to show the garden club. She has a real talent. She knows what the plants want. They will grow for her, I know. What a horror that was in Germany. Her German-ness is like a pane of glass between us. She is so good. I am attracted to the goodness in her, her way with plants, with her children, the way she keeps her house and her lovely large garden, but the horror is there. We both feel it. She told me once when we were collecting pine cones for xmas ornaments, that they had gone out gathering pine cones during the war, that they had no fuel and suffered from cold and hunger. I am afraid I grew silent and unresponsive, which is not my way to be, but the picture of the camps came between her and me. Once I heard or read of a German woman who lived not far from a death camp, who said that they cooked onions all the time to drown out the horrid smell from the camps. They knew and they did not know. They are so well behaved, so obedient, so able in practical matters. I love that in people, yet it can be dangerous at times. It *was* at that time.

June 3, 1980

We went to see the rose garden which is so beautiful right now that one does not feel in the ordinary world of the everyday at all. The roses now are bred to such colors, such shadings of flesh, yellow, pink and orange that they do strange things to the light, especially on a day when the air is full of moisture and the light tends to be colloidal anyhow. There is a shimmering of indeterminate color and heat and a fragrance. The whole garden is enclosed by lattice painted white and has an enclosed, dreamplace quality. We met Peter Mallon on the way out, and he said that people order their bones or ashes sent over to be put around certain bushes when they are cremated and that the bone meal is very good for the roses. He tells these macabre stories every time. I think they are part of his fantasy life. He speaks with a heavy German accent and is one of the world's foremost rose gardeners. I think of him as a rose in human form. What sort of dreams do roses have? They are, after all, the lions of the flower family, with their great thorns and their magnificent manes of brilliant color. They surely have cruel dreams.

Tuesday July 8, 1980

A muggy day. Some breeze though and not too hot. My roses, my lovely roses (John Ashbery roses, I call them in my mind) are out four and five at a time. Full of light, the color of flesh, shaded from pink to apricot to yellow, but pale, pale. I wish I knew their real name. Ravishing. This is a world full of unbearable beauty. I do not wish to leave it too soon, although the same thing must abide in our disintegration and reconstitution, I am sure. Some sort of similar delight must occur in worms and bacteria and whatever is to be made of me later. I have often thought that the enthusiasm must go back down to one's smallest component parts.

July 13, 1980

Today is a perfect day, clear sunny. Summer but not uncomfortably hot at all. The feeling of AIR around and in me so easy, so generative that it is something I keep in mind all through the rest of the year. "Dost thou know that fair land where the orange trees grow? Where the sun is like gold and etc." I sit on my back porch in a rocking chair and eat a cold, ripe peach. The rooms of my house are full of dispersed sunlight, a caring light, easy to live within.

May 20, 1981

Today is a cool, sunny day. The irises and weigelia, the flower of the horseradish, the violets and myrtle, the silver dollars and the gill-over-the-ground are all in bloom, all purple, pink and white. The backyard is green, blooming and neat in a shaggy way. Mine. My closed-in place where I sit on a peeling rocker as in paradise.

SPHERE REVOLVING LIKE A SKULL

Warm bear bounded by grain and bees
By the anatomy of seedplants and salmon

Unsteady fluid, model of the real
Our world, our dear edifice

Without dimension without parameters
Do not be vanquished by bad use.

Like ancient glass, enamels, glazed pottery
Stay long in your sands, under the loam

Beset by conflicts, paradox, fallacy
Full of evasion, pursued by falsity

Sphere, revolving like a skull
Dirty ice like the comets orbiting

Be busy with that motion we call heat.
Earth, earth, let your mantle crawl

With small creatures. Our chimera
Sphere revolving like a skull, live forever.

Stay. With your ill-posed problems
Your huge stones balanced in a circle

Of vector space. Sphere, our forcing bed
May your viscous mantle long be amnion
Membrane, cave and home for us.

BACK AGAIN, AGAIN

Seahorses coiling, uncoiling to move
The eggs carried
By the male in its pouch

Sharks, small ones, learning to raven
To tear bloody meat
Sharp and swift in their need

In the blue-green sea
The blue-green bays
Eyes open like fish

Nibbled and restored to bone
By small fish painted like eggs
By eels, companions to the lifting water

Or in the ploughed earth
Ready, moist
Stirring with bright worms

Open underneath for woodchucks, rabbits
Sweetened, kept fresh
By beetles, ants

Everyone lies down in it
Naked finally, unboxed, working back
Into the porous earth, the blue-green sea

Everyone, everything, returns
To the stuff, returns over and over
To the creatures of which it was made

THE YEARS

At the murky seabottom
Are ancient ships
With forgotten names
They are encrusted with history
History starts with two tiny leaves
On opposite sides of a tender stalk
Then come two larger leaves at right angles to the first two
This may be said to make a plus sign in green
Growing pluses larger and stronger each time

Consider coral how it grows
On drowned anchors of ancient Greek ships
Consider rust how it travels slowly
Into the anchor or the greenbronze hinges of ships
There are ideas, too, that have been grown upon
Like wrecks encrusted and softened

Great skill existed then in minting coins
Or making gold drinking cups. In these things
We see signs of the circularity and spiral growth
As on a see-saw the heavier weight must sit closer
To the fulcrum in order to achieve balance. "India is
Having terrible nightmares. The Chinese have walked
Into a cage." They weigh more but their feet
Cannot touch the ground. This is due to
The heavy shame of science on the
Other end of the board.
The lighter side has a
Heavier head.
It has taken a stone in its hand or a thick book
Still the growth although spiral is circular
When the year rolls around the leaves fall off
The motion of salt water, ebbing and flowing
The innumerable, microscopic corpses attaching themselves
To what lies in the grey depths finally rearrange
The weights so that now this side is up, now
The other. It is not a question of balance
But of time

RHIZOMES

At this time of the year
When the flags are about to flower
They must be covered by
A fine dusting of bonemeal
(Whose bones have been ground in
Is of no consequence)

The rhizomes are like tubers
Like potatoes, they spread
Under the soil. It is through
The growth of clumsy, twisted
Rhizomes in the soil
That they increase

Seldom through seeding
So the flowers are to look at
Or to smell, not for generation
Although there are those
Who are patient and skilled
Enough to crossbreed them
And make new kinds
New seeds

THE PREHISTORIC EMBRACE

There is a rightness about a horse pulling a cart.
It has been doing this sort of thing for a long time.

Horses in prehistoric times were as small as house cats
       with paws not hooves.
If they were made to draw a cart it would have had to be made
       of paper painted red with awnings of thin poppy-petals.

In my dream two men come to my door too early in the morning,
They have called for the contents of my basement,
With ease they remove a large box of broken plaster and tile,
       gears of stainless steel embedded in plaster.
They put it in a little wagon at the curb and expect the prehistoric
       horse harnessed to the wagon to pull it.

The horse is light-bodied with pleasure.
It is happy to pull such a burden, so out of proportion to
     its strength.
My anger awakens me. While I am not yet awake I resolve
     the dream
By lifting the animal up in my arms to protect it.
It snuffs at my face with delight.
We feel great tenderness for each other.

It is appropriate to get dressed up and dance at weddings
We take such comfort in the performance of ancient customs.
Old people cry at weddings because they know what
      wedded life and the passage of time can do.
Some guests go away hurt. They nurse their hurt feelings
      for decades.
There is always the widows' table. Not everyone can sit by the
      bride and groom.
The food may look like food but it is indigestible and not filling.

Everything is apt to be an imitation of itself,
In dreams we recognize this. We become indignant or full of fear.
We awaken to the warm embrace of the prehistoric, feel tender
      toward it.

Like the small prehistoric horse we tie ourselves to burdens way
      beyond our strength.
Those who have no need to run in pursuit of their daily prey
Run until they drop, smiling with satisfaction at how light
      their feet and bodies have become.
Delicate people with small bones lift and move loads of
      broken stone.
With bright-colored ribbons they harness themselves to
      mountains to pull until they die, triumphant.

Everything here is a replica. Nobody cries anymore. What is
      there to cry about?
Nothing is real. The widows are not widows. No one sits beneath
      the salt.

They are all dancing the dance of the bear, the camel, the monkey.
They are longing to be harnessed and made to be heroes.

SOLITUDE OF SALT

That Eden of the two-backed beast
Is in us yet. The ark we still have kept.

The eight legged pairs go up the ramp
In us. They have not left.

The rains come down in us.
The snake was he, the apple she.

The rain comes down like many feet
Our four and many eights.

We plunge, eyes shut, into the sea
A solitude of salt within us yet.

What is around us exists in us
Is in us still. The ark, the beasts, the rain.

The clocks and walls that tie us tight
Do not keep out the beasts and rain.

THE CLIMB

We stand in a cave
formed by the overhang of the waterfall
There is a curtain of thin waterstreams
coming down in front of us
It lets light through in
rainbow-filled droplets. The light is green
The air smells of water drying in sunlight
In front of the waterfall is a
slightly concave table of stone
On part of the table formed by water
is a half-inch deep pool, very bright
A frog sits in the center of the
sunlit pool. It gives off a wet, green-gold light
Its white underbelly lets through the sun
It pulses like a heart
We back away. We are silent
No girl will need to kiss this frog
No boy will take it home in his pocket
The people are silenced. They go behind the waterfall
There is a round embrasure
stone worn away by water
It is a frame through which branches grow
Each one leans through as through a window
Someone says he sees an eagle flying
in the space above the river
The river is a half mile down
It looks blue and gentle from this far up
The sun is going down
No one else can see an eagle
There are red peaks to either side
They are called OLD MAN, EAGLE

THE FIRST HOUSE WAS ROUND: 7000 B.C.

The cave had been a place
Inside of which they lived
It never had an outside

While they lived there, cave around them
The cave grew them within it
They both outgrew each other

The hidden cave that fed them
Could then no longer hold them
Their hut was built to take its place

They stood beneath the frightened sky
Piled stones all around them
Out where the grain would grow

They piled up stones for walls
A round cave built of stones
Where they could be inside
While their bread grew outside

THE COMPETENT KNIFE

Robust or slender (called gracile) they ground their food
And ground their teeth down doing it
They searched out seeds, roots, tubers
Following the great grazing beasts
Who were useful to them, and friends
Their differences less important than their similarities
The way, now, a dog will companion the cows
And bark when a heifer is in trouble
But were they hominid, human?
Were they made on the fifth day with the animals
Or on the sixth with *homo sapiens?*

(In Jamaica, far up in the hills
A small boy, twelve, maybe nine
Held a very large knife, a machete
Deftly slit an almond
Cut the top off a green coconut for a drink
Smiling, peeled a grapefruit
Which he scurried up a tree to get
And offered at the end of his knife
"How well you do that," his cousins said
Studying his sure eyes and the arm-long blade
Of his competent knife, dangerous
To coconut and fruit, not yet to kin.)

Their remains are found mainly in delta-mouths
Marshes, mud-flats, in shorezones of ephemeral character
They exploited the food on the fringes of the forest
The stream-valleys. Both the robust and gracile forms
Favored the more open vegetation at the edge of the shore
Because they needed to see danger coming

In Ethiopia, Kenya, Lake Rudolf, called Turkana
Along the Omo River, in the Afar Lowlands, in Olduvai Gorge
In the eastern rift of Tanzania, found with flint knives
Piles of fishbones, some bones of their friends the large grazers
And even, occasionally, bones of their cousins
        the Australopithicines
Who must have filled the gap when seeds, roots, tubers
(Not to mention coconuts and fruits, such luxuries as came later)
Were scarce and they were hungry.

GOOD MORNING, GOOD EVENING

Clean, they are. Good traders
       How much for this?
       One head.
       Won't you take forty strings?
       Bring on your cowries.
       Thirty?
       Bring on your money.
       Ten, then?
       Not a cowrie less. No.
The men with a little tuft of whiskers on the chin
A strip of hair left unshaven down the middle of the head.
The women with hands, fingers, nails and feet dyed red
The margin of the eyelids blackened
With sulphuret of antimony
A little powdered snuff on the tongue
Almost everybody, even the children

Acuare, they say. Good morning.
Acuale, they say. Good evening.
The superior person salutes first, saying *Acu.*
That is the name of their people, Acu.
The inferior says more. Adds a little to *Acu.*
Two persons, even strangers, very careful, scrupulous
Good morning. Good evening
Nothing interferes with this
"Anger draws arrows from the quiver
Good words draw cola-nuts from the bag."
The cola-nuts are bitter, slightly astringent
But not the Acu, not the Acu people
The young lie flat to the aged
Women kneel but do not lie down
Sons lie flat in front of their mothers
They may themselves be old already
Acuare, they say. Good morning.
Acuale, they say. Good evening.

AMERICAN GRANDCHILDREN

Everything but the garden fence
Iron colored Ukrainian grandmothers
Face to face, plain as a potato

Neurasthenic Welsh with rain-smoothed cheeks

Small Danish orphans, labelled and sent to the Mormons

Lost Seneca Indians with blue eyes

Japanese and Finnish lovers stewing together in hot baths

> Book with many pages all dripping honey
> America my baclava, macedoine, cous-cous
> Lovely America my stirabout, my ratatouille
>
> America you fat brown fig blushing in the hot blue
> Soft squash blossom, stony turnip, white lady-apple
> America my big purple cabbage, red ear of corn
> Full breast at which I suck and am sated
>
> Sky, wide sky, blue
>
> You spin straw into gold

Heart of a Thracian lion, eater of lambs, the American grandchild
"*Yaya*," she weeps, "I dreamt sad about *yaya*"

Eyes like black cherries, huge black olives
Sparrow-legs, kitten-paws
Whispers, with whispers she ties a wolf rides a wild horse.

*yaya— (Greek) grandma

SMARAGD THE EMERALD

The emerald, smaragd, protector of women
Binder of bowels, preventer of fits
Treasured by Cleopatra and Alexander
Worked intaglio by the ancient Greeks
      (Although in most languages
         the S before a consonant
         is used for a word of contempt
         as smear, snot, spit
         sbilenco—bowlegged
         smerdare—befoul)
Smaragdos the blue-green color
Crystals hexagonal, prisms breaking
On the basal plane imperfectly
At right angles to the geometric plane
Soft, not much harder than quartz
A low specific gravity, the cut stone
Not much brilliance or fire

The oriental emerald, green corundum
Lithia emerald miscalled hiddenite
Uralian emerald, demantoid
Brazilian emerald, green tourmaline
Evening emerald rightly a peridot
Pyro emerald, fluorspar
Mother of emerald, green quartz

From Muzo, Egypt, Etbai
Jebel Sikait, Jebel Zabara
Near the Red Sea east of Assuan
Bogota, Colombia, Peru, Coscuez, Smondoco
Found in the Urals
On the shores of the Takovaya River
In Habachtal of the Salzburg Alps
In Eidvold, Norway
Found in mica schist in talc schist
In nests of calcite in black bituminous
Limestone containing ammonites
Of lower cretaceous age
Associated with quartz, dolomites, pyrites
Found in mica schist with aquamarines
Alexandrite phenacite and beryl

Taken internally
Smaragd, the emerald is good for the eyesight
Worn on the person it is a help
Against epilepsy a cure for dysentery
Assists women in childbirth
Keeps away evil spirits
Preserves chastity

THE CITY THE WALLS

The city and its houses
Foundations and walls
I destroyed burned with fire

The wall the outer wall
Temples and gods
Temple towers of brick and earth
As many as there were I razed
And dumped into the Arahtu canal

I dug canals through the city
I flooded it with water
I caused the earth of it
To be taken up in baskets
I had it carried down to the Euphrates
To be washed away to the sea

      What Sennacharib and his jackals
      What the close cropping goats and sheep
      Had made dust
      We gathered together
      With the living roots
      Of eucalpytus trees
      Brought from far places

      We cradled the soil
      For pomegranates and grains

      We held the water in our palms

      Wept into it
      Mixed it with our own scant moisture
      Listened to the cry of the dust
      Moistened it with our fasting saliva
      Our long hunger

      We dug up the old stones
      We made a new city a new wall

COLD WIND TUNE GONE

Strong! You were to me
A brother and sister of the north sort
We played, threw a stick in the northern way

You sang loud and hot, magic songs
Your joy in life, your rough jokes
Like a tiger-cub full of golden juice
You dared. You'd hunt at home
The rick was a kingdom

The mist smelled strong of sky
Thirty hot days we had there
There we sat. In sitting dreamt
Of summer springs bubbling all the long days
All the long day our eyes drank shade

Sit here too my sister
I want to sink in wide islands
New to me as bragging brook
Dig through to home here

After the fading of summer colors
Her heart ate great work
Strong! In the woods I listened
All day to her song

She put her faith in height
There were some ends boiling. She was
Making bread blossom in salty, warm sun
In the heat I covered her with pine cones
Berryblooms, little fruits and nuts

Fall weather under her first wingtrial
Big, she was, by first Fall
When cold came again from the north
To bludgeon her eagle-stead with wind

THE OTHER

Looking at the powdery mildew on the leaves,
I see a twig turn
and study me.
First one eye and then the other.
It holds its head, a triangle, on a proud neck
as I do.
I breathe carefully
and, gentle, I submit.
It holds the branch with delicate green hands
and is aware of me.
We know one another.

In the sea, far out, I am alone with a gull.
Its yellow, bare eye looks carefully at me.
With intelligent wings it finds firmer air
and floats over and around.
It dips and curtseys
now rests like a toy on the waves.
The yellow eye is a place.
It invites me.

But when I catch a hornet and hold it
frightened
in a loose fist
to send it back to its accustomed air
It stings my palm
Because I am outside
and too close.

HOLDING HIS BRANCH

Holding his branch
And trembling
At small terminations
In the grass below
His ears turn tremble

Silent in a corridor
Of awareness
He is completely
Perceptive
To the presence
Of not-being
Not-holding

On the point of attention
Always
Attentive with terror
He is aware

Resigned finally
Accepting the ending
Of his need to fear
To be attentive

INCHWORM

There is a listening the inchworm does
With his advancing foot
Trying the air around a leaf
For possibility

Shaped like a U upside down
He waves his advancing foot
(His eyes and ears are in it)
He decides by stretching out flat
to straighten the loop of his back
Then brings the other foot closest again
To start to listen again

Often he retraces his steps
Seeking as painfully backward
Or drops from a leaf by a thread

At the end of his rope
He sways in the breeze
Until chance catches him
To ride where others decide

152

THIS IS HIS MEAT

Lingers sniffing
Lips parted
Eyes half shut

Finds blueberries
At a pure pitch
Picks with lips only
Bursts on the palate
Blue with slow tongue
His meat

Eats besides this
Only moths
Green-white
Lofts easily
He seizes mid-air

Grows light in weight
Smells blue like
A flower his breath
Not thick or bloody

Moth-like himself
Weightless he springs
Poised in air slowly
He turns and floats
Down with a moth
Unhurt in his lips

THE CAT WHO ATE HER KITTENS

There was a cat who ate her kittens
All but one
She loved them so

Then
She walked up and down
In front of her remaining kitten
Her hair on end with rage

She was sure someone would
Come and eat him
She did not know exactly who

MOON

Bearing pins, magnets, rounded garments
floating threads of blue.
Buoy in the night
Bell of unknown guests

Periodic burden of us all
Neaptide and springtide
Low and full
Calendar of women

Their feet bound and hobbled
Thighs tangled, interlaced
Blood pulled, shackled
By moonlight.

LLAMA

The llama is not unwilling
It will carry great burdens
But if overloaded will sit down
Or spit

Is curious
So interested in phenomena
It will stay to be shot
Rather than miss the opportunity
To observe

Prefers to die with others of its kind
Its bones being found in great heaps
Although the llama is never ridden
It is not insolent, but other

It does not crowd the space of its herders
Mountain dwellers
Valuing their privacy
Decorate the llama with bright woolen
Apples

It looks far along its nose but sees best
Inward
Does not appreciate companionship other
Than llamas

DOG-SHARK

The dog-shark floats belly up
spoil of surfeit
his reticent curves
dented lightly
by virtuoso thumbs
thunder's pup speeding neat to havoc
stony dark, shaped tight for ravening
unstrung by plenty.

Piked and thorny
his hide rasps our palms
as air stings and revives him
to beat the bilge with rage
tooth tooth all tooth
and hurt.

The sea our sewer his Cockaigne
spicy with blood and detritus
buttered his gills
mellowed the trap in his jaw
so he lies in the boat belly up
smiling slightly
weanling assassin
debauched.

COUNTING THE BIRDS

a scorner
a watcher
a screecher
a warner
a crested commander
a blue demander
a four colored blue
a jay

a tree top caller
a fire
a green dusted fire
a crier
a crested sayer
a ten time prayer
a two a pair
bright fallers
quiet hoppers
a fair pair

a touhee
a touhee
a four color bird
a three color bird
a one eye a one eye
a stare on the stair
an imp
ertinent hopper
a stopper a stayer
a one eye a touhee
a thrasher
a scraper
a searcher a lurcher
a red brown thrasher

a focus in motion
a leaf mold searcher
a brown leaf thrasher
a ground watcher
a searcher for motion
a brown thrasher
a pair
a true crew
a nodder a prodder
a weaver
a figure eight dancer
a crew of two
a true trait
a constant mourner
two mourning doves
two

DOG

Eager
he leaps
falls flat
and slides on his chin
turns over
smiles
and yawns
scratches
but misses the itch
hits instead his
surprised nose
bites the foot
finds it's his own
licks his stomach
for comfort and
washes well
at the bottom
slides over unbalanced
and sleeps
one hind foot still
up in the air.

OLD CAT

My cat died
who floated airy
over fences
ran lightly on surmises
mocked architecture
and gravity

whose stare
deeply yellow
probed silence
tasting warmth
hummed rounds
of quiet
to the Place

studied salt air
milkweed blossom, roses
lofted tiptoe
crossed his eyes
and squirted musk
on honeysuckle

focused inward
burned an exit
through the center

MY FAMILIAR

Although dead two years
And taken away by the trash man
In a large brown bag
My old familiar hums like a top
Warm near my feet by the sink.

No hunger nor cold brings him
Waxing like the moon
But the place, the still spot
Where the top spins round
Which I fix for him
And offer like fish.

CIRCUS BEAR LOST

How shall I suffer the sunlight
And the fierce penetration of berries
Shaped as I am to the comfort
Of musty cages around me?
I go with my eyes looking backward
Out of fear of leaves moving freely.

Tie me.

How can I sleep in the open
Owned by the click of the beetles
Working on corpses beneath me?

Watch how I stand on my head and I balance.

Watch me.

Having lost my accustomed companions
Cozy around me in trouble
I stand in a clearing and dance
My old waltz—

Watch me waltz in the unfamiliar air of the forest.

Feed me.

THE GARDENER CAME

The gardener came
and untwisted the woodbine
(or was it bittersweet)
where it curled around the oak.

Some branches
he had to cut
the stubborn oak had braided
where the vine insisted.

Winters they tossed red bells
companionable together
unsolemn.

Alone the oak stands dark
apart from houses.
Its dry leaves rattle
while the bittersweet
tries to find a staff
in wild cherry, forsythia
wild rose
seeking with trembling tendrils
dragging down the weak growth
it sends a thousand shoots
curling and turning on rock
on grass, on earth, on air itself
into the community of lilacs
over the dead wood of shacks.

The lonely bells ring all over the hillside
for a remembered stubbornness.

In the changeless evening
of its own oneness
the oak stands bare
growing hard
among the easy birches

IN A SMALL AND FRIENDLY JUNGLE

In a small and friendly jungle
of dead bicycles, torn paper and weeds,
where I wait in the new morning air,
I saw a rat,
thin and trembling with cold,
glean the remains
of carnival suppers,
tossed aside the night before
in their gay wrappings
to wait

for the widowed sparrow
the orphaned gull
and the poor,
we have always with us.

STOP, THIEF

The small leaflings at the edge of each leaf
Tear them off. Distribute them on new soil.
All my days and nights torn away (Stay, thief)
Giving out apples and cholla, plain toil.
There are only so many days. They coil
In circling hours. "I have only two hands."
The squirrels are busy. The birds too, spoil
The trees of cherries. They make stands
Against the time of day, time's sands.

THE BIG FLOOD OF THE SEINE, 1910

The water sent up by the flood
Good for trees and leaves
But not for stalls full of books

Tore the books off the stalls
Piled them up like fish scales
Like shingles on a roof

In a pattern which looked haphazard
Books, ideas, order in disorder
The people of Paris were astonished

Thomas Aquinas lay over Byron
Chaucer and Emerson intermingled
Cookbooks and books on metallurgy

When they dried, the pages stuck
The bindings curled together
So that lead and chromium

Omelets and smoked ducks
Ruffled and twisted together
In a new order, an organization
As witty and chancy as water

V

January 28, 1980

This morning I was rereading for the one-hundredth time, *Three Poems* by John Ashbery. In Israel, when we had nothing else to turn to, I found it enough for two weeks of uninterrupted rereading. Over and over, it never loses its charm. Like the prayers which I did not comprehend except in moving darts of light, I find it not plain as a whole but true in unconnected flashes. The whole tone is LIGHT, more like brook water than an angry river but how it catches the light of day. The collaging of weather-talk, asides and intimations of great woe, lightly brushed in, are endlessly fascinating. I cannot look away for fear of missing some *Key* to the understanding of the message. There is purposely no message. Not actually written in.

When J.A. was small his mother said, when he went to another boy's house, "Do not overstay your welcome." He writes like that. His poems never overstay their welcome. They change in passing so that it is as if another person has come in to take the place of the one who first visited. I study the rooms of his poems. It comes to me that anyone might be short-patienced enough to say, as some critics do, "The rooms are empty. There is no one and nothing there." There are. The rooms are full of moving light and shadow. They are full of space within a small confine. No one outstays his welcome.

January 30, 1980

The richest ideas are in works of philosophers or historians who are more or less unconscious of the language in which they express their conclusions. Then the language is remarkably *anschtendig*— how to translate my meaning for that?— respectable won't do, solid, together, unassuming, non-literary. "No statues," as Yves Bonnefoy said. I think it was he. No statuary in the language of the poem. The most difficult thing for me to swing. My education was bad in that respect. I had a capability which deserved better education than it got.

February 3, 1980

Today I went to hear William Bronk read. He reads in a strange way— not like his poetry, which is modest, although it is full of hidden virtuosity. His reading is orotund, full of mellow overtones, strangely theatrical. His poetry is simple, not literary, usually, but full of philosophical depth. Byways of the mind, Labyrinthine.

171

A strange thing happened. He read a poem for me, said so, but I thought he was looking at someone in the first row. Jacob said no, he looked at me. I went up to tell him how masterful the poem CONJUGATION was—I guess I had written him about it—and he leaned toward me resting his forehead against mine. I once dreamt that I did that to John Ashbery. When I told John about it, that I wanted some of his inspiration to come into my head that way—he shook his head no and looked a little frightened. His dreams are his. No one else may share them. He needs all of them. Bronk is more generous with his dreams. Write to me, he says, here, and gives the address.

Coming home I was very melancholy because of the nature of Bronk's writing, so quietly hopeless, so plainly despairing. Still, I was high at the same time.

Monday April 14, 1980

Yesterday was so beautiful a day that I spent a good part of it outdoors in the 70 degree sunlight, enjoying the neighbors' children and the neighbor, while I tried to read some of Harold Bloom's *Blake's Apocalypse.* I get a new and different insight into Blake's prophetic works from what I had when I was young and felt a complete identity with Blake. We are not so much alike. He is male and not of the Bible people. He lived a simple, hard-working life with not much reward for his labor and genius while he lived, but he was against all custom and rule, "Newton and Locke" were anathema to him. The Greeks with their MEASURE and the Hebrews with their LAW, were his enemy. The Devil was Memory vs Divine Imagination. I see in Blake theoretical ragings which did not show themselves in the way he lived his life. Yet there still is a similarity. I live in a "moony cave" and am the Female Will, which he abhorred; but since he was always showing the Emanation to be of the opposite sex of his gods and hierarchies, perhaps, in that sense I am like Blake. The innocence of sexual delight is an idea which I took from his writings when I studied them in my late teens. He did not live that way having only his Catherine, nor did I, having only had Jacob, but in my stance toward people who do live that way he influenced me.

172

May 1, 1980

We went to the Guggenheim and saw a large show of the works of Chillida, a Basque sculptor. His works are frequently fitted together like a three-dimensional jig-saw puzzle, with I-beams, mortise and tenon, and other holding forms. He works chiefly in iron, but uses alabaster also—very beautiful and unexpected for such forms, like large, translucent geodes with strange cities inside, the square and rectangular forms within the cleanly sliced off rocks of alabaster contrasting in texture and shape. Very mystical, somehow.

Perhaps I say so because I know the Basque people to be a people different from others, with powers of transcendence not as usual to other "civilized" peoples. It is peculiar how these beliefs, fears really, about certain sections of country come into currency. Transylvania, Basque country, Ireland; the Jews, the pygmies, and they are people who are not assimilable into the general mass, not altogether assimilable, because of course there are many who do disappear into the amorphous generality of the places to which they go. The Basque language is not a Sanskrit derivative as are most known languages. Nor is it Dravidian, like Turkish, Hungarian and Latvian. It is of unknown origin.

The sculptures are (more recently) compact with semicircular "arms" of iron, wood, cast-concrete or ceramic. Earlier on they had many branches of square-sided iron reaching out. Some were called "air combs," appropriately. To some of the earlier works, he gave literary names, like "Clamor of Limits," "Anvil of Dreams." The later pieces are more "together." The extensions become part of the whole form—within a shape of the iron or within the limits of space taken by the whole piece. It is amazing work, marvelously virtuoso in the making of the material object and at the same time mysterious, archaic. Although the work is part of the time like Giacometti, Brancusi and whoever it was in the late fifties that started iron sculpture as *menace*. The iron maiden theme?

I enjoyed the encounter with someone unknown to me before this. It is a marvel how a large body of work by one artist teaches the art of that one so well. I do not enjoy group shows as much. I suppose I am not enough a quick learner. My memory can not retain the special quality of each of all the artists in the group. Sometimes one artist in a group will stick in the memory, maybe not the most honest artist of the group either, just the most easily recalled.

There was a group show of Spanish artists with the Chillida retrospective. In it I noticed especially an artist by the name of Zush (an Israeli?). He or she is somewhat like Samaris, but much more shocking. The artist uses Hebrew script as drawings and as embellishments in the background of paintings, which are made up of many small paintings on one canvas, like comic strips, exceedingly pornographic and shocking. There are figures bleeding, giving birth, with striped erect penises, dissolving, disintegrating etc. All of this is decorated in dots and tiny decorations of primary or secondary color and black, like Moroccan embroidery. The contrast of the skilled but childlike drawing and the horrifying subject matter has a true fairytale quality of terror and fascination. This one remembers—how not?

May 9, 1980

I got a call from John Ashbery today. He is going to Poland at the request of Washington, which is paying for and arranging the whole tour. They are to visit Auschwitz and have a picnic there!? He does not know if he will take advantage of that part of the trip. They will be in Cracow and several other places. He and Susan Sontag and Joyce Carol Oates and Saroyan; a peculiar mixed bag but being so able, all of them, and open to experience and what it connotes, exactly, they will, I am sure, have an interesting trip with each other, different though they may be.

June 1, 1980

This morning at breakfast I was re-reading THE INNER THEATER OF FRENCH POETRY by Mary Ann Caws. It's very much a professorial effort. There are none of the quirky, skewed logics of Harold Rosenberg's sort. It plows and plods, but I, I take off from it, flying like a bat in jagged, erratic sallies from one thought to another. This is a joy to me—*the* joy.

Anyone reading the poems of the modern French sees what has taken the place of metaphor in their work and in ours—Stevens, Ashbery and all their flocks of small birds, following them in the air. There are patterns evolving, highsigns. From a distance, with my dreamlike memory everything becomes an amalgam. It is a borrowing from the thought-patterns of madness. It too becomes smooth and boring after a while. "The deliberate shimmering presence" and "the western glory of an institution of death" and "it is the step left behind oneself, the track circling a great empty region, not to be entered but which is the place." (All quotes from Yves Bonnefoy.) This sometimes gives me IDEAS, especially the last quote. But often these are ornaments on a casket. *I* shall have a plain pine box, made with no nails, slightly open so the small worms and beetles can "take of my body and eat" as they say. My greatest passion all my life has been to FEED: people and animals. It makes me part of that larger world, the world with no words, the one with acts.

September 28, 1980

I read a review of *As We Know* by John Ashbery in *Parnassus*. It is by William Harmon, a professor at Chapel Hill, North Carolina. It is a hysterically unfavorable review, insulting, unnecessarily abrasive. Jealousy, frustration, are the motivation behind such an ugly piece of writing. The water must be allowed to carry you or your sink, which causes sputtering, choking. Such vixenish spitting and snarling, dear, dear. And everybody who likes Ashbery gets it in the neck too. Harold Bloom, David Shapiro, David Kalstone, David Lehman, all no good, says W. Harmon from his eminence in Chapel Hill, North Carolina. Shoo.

May 20, 1981

I got, from Gotham, SHADOW TRAINS by John Ashbery. Fifty short poems (short for him, not for me) of four quatrains each. Sixteen lines each in which he casts away, casually, his mayblooms. They are SO young. I feel they are written to and for me. His poems are intransitive. That is why so many reviewers of his work become angry and unfair. His admirers are happy to be the non-object of an intransitive verb. How much love, throwaway love, there is in them for any person who is willing to hang loose and bask in this unspecific love. I like, especially, if I were forced to pick among favorites, "Paradoxes and Oxymorons":

This poem is concerned with language on a very plain level.

The language here is on a very plain level, but as he says, it plays. And what is play? The playfulness of Hermes, I think. Sacred.

What an honor to have had that time of his workshop and the informality of being with him for a whole year. It is a very democratic world we live in. A cat may look at a king, may sit under his chair.

175

In my mind I write him letters about his work and prayerfully, I wish him well. How does God go about his work of bestowing blessings? I was not brought up to think that such a life as Ashbery has led would be so rewarded, in work as in his person. Yet from the beginning—consider David, a man of blood, committing adultery, unfaithful to his king and his best friend, the king's son, the most blessed of poets and rulers, the maker of Jerusalem, the shaper—with Moses—of a people. Art is the answer. Maybe God is enchanted with those whom he favors *because* he has favored them. "I choose whom I choose," says He. Just so. Just because, that's why! While "Job sat in a corner of the dump, eating asparagus/ with one hand and scratching his unsightly eruptions/ with the other." Just because. Why, then, am I so happy? It is like the flowers in May. It comes in its time for no reason. And goes away leaving me just as sad and grey for no reason either. Poetry is bread. I live in a house of bread. I eat very plain food on a very plain level. It is good.

MY MOTHER

(translated from the Hebrew of Haim Nagid)

Among our flocks of hard days
My mother padded about in soft slippers
(Aaron Aaron
Her voice bleached white in the streets.)

I found gleaming pearls in my dresser drawer
One of my mother's relics.
My days were quietly severed
From the silence of her pearl-perfect life.

Brought to the ground by the rage of my days
I attach myself to her memory.
Like a soft rain it pours dimness on me.

In my sleep flags of blackness
Are folded and put away.

THE ROOM

The room
I rented for a hen's egg
Ivy covered and with jalousies
In the quarantine quarter

The old woman, my landlady
Finally starved to death
In her overstuffed parlor

The winter was so cold
They moved cannon over the frozen river

In the quarantine quarter
The water-pump was its greatest treasure

Surrounded by women
Their water-pails filled to the brim
Covered with twigs
To form a hard-frozen lid
While they rushed back to their rooms nearby
Before it would all freeze

Always the old woman cleaned her house
As if she were about to die
She purified it

The houses were clay-walled
There were clay fences as tall as a man
Labyrinths of clay, narrow alleys
A mortuary, cold
There was a smell of baking bread
Of kerosene lamps

She kept me like her bird
Cleaned my cage, scattered crumbs
Cooked me a meal of potatoes, onions
A handful of rice

Salted with stars, a frozen clay sepulcher
A pestilence, a thirty-year war
Frost, barking dogs, silent houses
They had been bundled in and brought here
Transported in closed cars like captive birds

(after Osip Mandelstam)

LAMENT FOR THE QUIET GIRL

After a love poem in hieroglyphs

I need to fly
Like all those different birds
By night, by starlight
Untwist the rope that ties me
And go to the death-boat with you
Like a hawk above it
Like the sun sending away the dark
Like a cloud full of rain

I am cut down like grain
O girl seated quiet in the boat of the dead
The weight of grief in my sack is too heavy

I lay in my bed at night
And thought of a house for us both
With the long-legged cranes nearby
And a boy playing outside with a bowl and stick

O broken bowl, torn sail, faithful stork
Lark, flying out of sight and calling my name
The scythe cuts me
The sun has gone under. My house is dark
The water-jug is broken
The bread-bowl is empty
My life is too long

MANICHAEAN PRAYER (freely adapted)

The Light

> Shine God
> Do you
> In me
> Make peace
>
> Light bringer
> Redeem my soul
> From this born-dead
>
> O new moon
> And spring
> Lord
>
> Praise
> We praise
> Light   shine-God
>
> Make peace
> Light bringer
> Virgin of light
>
> New blessing may come
> O moon and spring
> Light bringer
> Shine here
> Lord
>
> Star
> Good faith
> Glittering
>
> Star of light Mar Mani
> Teacher of the east
> Redeem my soul from
> In me make peace
> O light-bringer
> From borndead redeem us

The Dark

> Mixed light
> Darkness and light
> Praise and light
> Light and darkness
> Of various earths
>
> Libidinous prince
> Elements of darkness
> Demon serpent
> Held captive by light
> Sun
>
> Held captive
> By moon thighs
> Dark prince
> Demon serpent
> By the bright limbs
>
> Releasing light
> In moony limbs

THE SPIRIT IS LIKE THAT

Spirit is made of infinitely small particles
When the spirit leaves the body, the body appears the same
A breath, a warmth, has left it. That was the spirit

In fear of death the man with bad spirit takes his own life
Because of fear of life's end he lingers forever in the doorway
    of death
He piles wealth on wealth. He kills. He laughs at a
    brother's death
Is made sick by another's glory
Accumulates worthless trinkets, old toys, titles, prizes
His mind, made dark by the darkness of spirit, hates sunlight

So he breaks old friendships by talebearing and lies
Scoffs at sincerity. Is nauseated by it.
Trembles and starts with fear at nothing
His spirit is dark. His mind is dark. His body is sick
His flesh hates itself. It sweats. His face is pale,
    his speech broken
His voice fails. There are tears in his eyes. He falls down

Why can he not understand that death is like pissing
Let him consider what happens when he sleeps
Full of ease, untied, his body lies loose
Something else remains awake, open to joy and sorrow
When the arm is cut off the fingers still grasp. They itch
Life forsakes the veins and abandons the bones but not
    the spirit
Do not say that the body, the mind and the spirit are
    in harmony
Harmony is for musicians. Let them keep that word. We do
    not need it
The force that guides the body well or poorly is in the body
Here is the source. The caressing touch. Joy when no one
    is near
No one touches. The spirit touches

Spirit is so fine it seems a breath, a warmth only
Not the mind. The mind can look on any horror
The mind can react with opposite motions, laughing at sorrow
Water flows easily down. Honey not. It is sticky and
    flows slowly
A pile of poppy seeds can be moved by a breath
The spirit is like that

(After Lucretius)

THE SELF

To conceive the self
To carry and beget the self
As a creature not an idea

By perfect insight to know
Up and down, through and through
The self as a body, as flesh

To be born in self before dying
Learn to be quiet, keep silent
Be at peace so that small words
Can be heard from a distance
And acted upon as they are heard

But if you say
There is nothing but idea
What would there be to long for
What creature, what perfect being
What essence, what brew of self?
(Idea comes between
Self and self
There is no oneness)

This brewing of virtue
Which emanates like a vapor of silence
This movement toward perfection
Acting for good until it is acted upon
Longs for a word not its own
To be spoken to it and out of it

The flesh longs to forget things
And ideas which surrounded and stuffed it
Up until now
To be in the body wholly now
Until a word sounds from elsewhere
Without idea, wholly in oneness
Wholly in the body

The spirit also denies the body
It withdraws to perfection
(Which does not exist)
It has no use for memory or intelligence
Which are of the body

The warmth and energy of the body
Physical, not idea
May fly from the storm now
May hide for a time
But when the word sounds finally
In the true quiet, the silence
The intrinsic self will be made one
Again one self

(After Meister Eckhart)

CONVERSATION WITH RILKE
ABOUT DRAGONS

Sicknesses
That are superficially and foolishly handled
Withdraw
After a pause
They break out again more fearfully
They are unlived, spurned
Lost life of which one may die

Perhaps if we knew
We would then endure our sorrows
With greater confidence than our joys
For they are moments when
Something new has entered into us
Something unknown

      When I was so sad
      Those times when I seemed to attract
      Misfortune
      It was because I had built this destiny up
      Myself
      By my past, my special character
      So peculiarly suited to misfortune

Our feelings grow mute
In shy perplexity
Everything in us withdraws
A stillness comes
And the new which no one knows
Stands in the midst of it
And is silent
      My future stood before me
      Waiting for me to move up into it
      Silent

Only because so many
Have not absorbed their destinies
While they were living in them
And transmuted them into themselves
They have not recognized
What has gone out of them
      Now I write myself
      My own letters of condolence
      I am open and patient
      With sadness
      Ready to help it out
      Of myself

THE MOTHER, THE OLD MOTHER

What is the mother
What do you think
The great mother
The hope of the human race?

Yes   The damp earth
There lies joy for men

Every earthly woe
And every earthly tear
Is a joy

When you water the earth
With tears a foot deep
You will rejoice
At everything at once
Your sorrow will be no more

I've taken to kissing the earth
At my prayers
I kiss it and weep

There is no harm in those tears
Even if there is no grief
Tears flow from joy

What I weep for most
Is my baby
I had a baby with tiny nails

My only grief is
I can't remember it

When it was born
I wrapped it in cambric and lace
I put ribbons on it

I strewed it with flowers
I took it away through the forest
I was afraid
I was frightened of the forest
I took it to the pond

If it is not so
If I never had that baby
(Perhaps I didn't)
I cry for it anyway

(After a passage from Dostoyevsky's
The Possessed)

YVES BONNEFOY

After I learned how to embroider I learned
how to remove all adornment. This was the

second simplicity, but my imperfections were me.
By meeting the menace of final immobility

I enfolded the threat of silence. I sent away
stones, ships, salamanders, summer stars.

This salamander is a sudden, strange monster.
It appears from nowhere and disappears without sound.

It is a gift not asked for, taken as due,
now lost in a long silence, a desert.

Because order and rest do not go with breathing fire
nothing is what I am about from now on. Dry sand

the desert, a stone. This is not *hier*, yesterday.
It is for good. The foliage of the dead

written on by the passing seasons, the stone marker
called *borne* at the edge of the path. It is a

bourne from which no traveler returns.
It is a sign of absence. There is no word

no wind. The small red dragon on the wall
is gone. My mouth is filled with earth

with emptiness. "Jour du parole ... nuit de vent"
gone. I face the immobility in stillness.

In removing the imperfections I removed all,
thinking that images were no longer of use

at a certain depth. Does "a bird cry like a sword?"
for me like many razors. I am covered with

small cuts but they are dry. They no longer
flow words by day, poems at night.

ALL SNOWED UNDER

Lermontov, darling, get out of my head
I am all snowed under like Russia
Honey drips out of my nose like snot

Those songs of yours my mother sang me
As she rocked me in the oak rocking chair
Put me to sad sleep like violins

The girls drinking vinegar, spitting blood
Shedding causeless tears by the window
Death in the snow sweet as raspberry tea

The heat of the porcelain stove
The tongs with red coals for the samovar
Packs of wolves singing like gypsies
        Dear Sir,
            When you send me a rejection slip
            Send one also to Mikhail Yurievich
            Lermontov
            who is either in Moscow
            Or in the army in the Caucasus.
            His poems have no bite. (Although
            His sword cuts well enough)
            He has no leaps except into an early
            Grave. His poems are fit only to be
            Sung by girls dying for love in the
            Long Russian winter.
                        Yours,
                        R.D.
Yurievich my melancholy mirror
Our tears make us cry. How we love them, we Russians
Get out of my head. It's slushy. The mud is three feet deep.

AFTER MARTIAL FREELY

Bark if you choose
Wherever we meet
Spray dirty insults mixed with spit
You will be denied this fame for certain
Which you sought through my verses
To be known through the world
Now you are known to be, somewhere
But unknown you shall die, you misery
This is necessary
There may be some, even a few
Who might bend down to stroke
Your slimy pelt
I will withhold my fingers from this sore

AFTER CATULLUS

(60)

You lioness from the terrible mountains
You death-monster, barking with your bottomless cunt
Now shall I plead with you on my knees
In my latest turn of bad luck
Or shall I loathe you forever
After suffering so much from you
My own darling heart

(52)

What's wrong, Catullus?
What have you got against dying?
Will that cancer N sit in the seat of power
Will V lie himself blue in the face for high office
What's wrong Catullus?
What have you got against dying?

(53)

Somehow or other the rabble
Smile and marvel as my Calvus
Brings false charges out in the open
As he makes things plain and straight
They are hands-out in admiration
At the Dimension of this midget orator

A SONG OF LERMONTOV

I go out alone
The road is wide. It glitters
With a fine ash of frost

Quiet night. The wilderness
Hears God's speech
The stars sing His praise

The sky is deep, distant
It stops the heart
The earth rests in a blue glow

Why am I so full, so full
Of heavy longing
Am I waiting for someone
Have I spoiled something
Something I gambled and lost?

No. I wait for nothing
Nothing more from life
And the next life
Is not what I fear

I long to rest to be released
To leave all this, to sleep
Not the cold sleep
Not death not the tomb

I long for sleep that lasts
My breast forever moving
My soul beating, stirring

Day and night to hear a song
A song of love without an end
Always new always beginning

A tree whose boughs
Bend and rustle
A green and leafy song over me

(After a version in Yiddish)

CRAZY ARI AND THE MOON

Oh, Moon, Moon
See how you lie in a puddle
And shine
Moon, Moon

But if you lay in the mud
Like crazy Ari
Lies in the mud
You would not shine
Moon, Moon

(Translated from the Yiddish of an actual
shtetl *character remembered by RD's mother)*

YIDDISH SONG

For what's away, is gone, is not here
Far away that hour, that early year
How fast my young luck flew away
And no one can bring it back today
For what's away is away, is not here

Who runs now to serve me, to empty my heart?
Do I talk out of my senses?
It's because of the smart
I suffer a sickness not really called sick
They call it old age. It came here so quick
Because what's away is away, is not here

THE MILLER'S TEARS

The little boy is crying
He hears the leaves crying

No. The tree is not crying
It is singing a song about rain

      The boy is comforted
      His mother holds him in her lap
      She strokes his cheek
      She sings him an old song

      From the time of her grandparents
      It is called "The Miller's Tears."
      No, she says, The Tree is not crying
      It is singing about rain.

      She sings about the miller
      How he came to the mill
      When his hair was black
      The wheel turned. Now he is grey

      And old. No one is crying
      They are singing about the wind
      How no one sees it
      And about rain

SESTINA IN HOMAGE TO HUEY KAI KWONG

(for John Yau)

Up and down my needle flashes in the sun.
I draw it through the canvas, followed
By colors which gradually form a plan.
When I start I do not know what is to come.
Each color asks for each, so the woolen roses grow.
It all depends on what I have on hand.

A bit like Huey's turning of his hand
Making a paper-thin clay bowl, large as the sun.
The clay he shaped shaped itself. His fingers followed
But it was his past, his history made the plan.
Almost against his will he made perfection come
And then, a little, he would spoil it, not let it grow.

Five thousand years of patience made it grow
His people coaxing patience like rice shoots in the hand
(without effort no perfection under the sun)
So many bowls destroyed, sixty, a hundred, this followed.
So many templates carved by hand before this plan
The many that he broke before to make ease come

That let the perfect, pliant clay build and come
That let the mound of clay find its centerpoint and grow.
His thinking fingers, sentient palm, wise hand
The skin a sunlit color, warm like sun
Almost too skilled, with something of despair that followed
His eye and touch that grew the living plan.

His intention was to make a bowl. The wheel made the plan.
If the wheel would not obey the shape would never come.
Sometimes he would be sad, only perfect forms would grow.
He would have to run a flaw in with a sliding of the hand.
He was too blessed, born on a day all sun.
He longed for the struggles of his art, the joy that followed

When he broke bad bowls and good ones followed
When his skill was difficult, when he balanced on the plan
Until by force and repetition his easyhanded art would come
And like a melon a bowl would grow.
Then he was content to give no care to his hand
But let the shapes grow magic in the sun.

The yellow sun it was that followed Huey
Its ancient gift that made his great gift come
That made clay grow supple and shining from his hand.

ARP

Here fades the edge
of bird in leaf
of egg in flight
convex-concave
within a cloak
the two or three
are one to stroke.

It twists to face itself
it feeds the stone within
itself a turning
feeding fed
of glowing breast or groin.

A cup of figs
a place of pears
throat of horse
shaved head of boy
a shell a dimpled egg.

A dream thrusts out the bronze
of princess long asleep
with fishes
floating linen and
sea smooth stones.

Powdersnow
slow dancers of crystal
sleep-seeds starting.

WHERE IS THE DOPPELGANGER?

Where is the Doppelganger
Able to lose himself in another
Who comes and joins the creature
That hides in the skin of the poet

His eyeballs rolled back
White and not seeing
Hardly breathing, dazed
Clinging to dark corners

Disappearing over sunlit waves
Like a pair of linked dragonflies

Able to listen together
In darkness and hear distant words?
All around and inside silence
Silence

TO JOHN YAU

Stop burbling into your inscrutable mustaches
If you don't get up on top of the spruce tree
And sing out loud and clear
Someone will take over your tree
You golden-spotted, red-capped, yellow-throated
Sapsucker you.

BEARINGS ON THE ROTHENBERG SHIELD

Matthew, mild and merry
A new man at
Tephillin-laying time
(Time returned to us)
Hand and arm tied on the side of the heart
Easy, ebullient, eager, his
Wand warm, he is

Ripening, ready, the new Reb Rothenberg, an
Offshoot of the open-handed Jerry
There with good deeds at the right time,
Holds his hilt high
Eden is his
Natural element, a young
Buck, his body buoyant
Earthy, effective. He
Responds, is real as a
Garden, generous, a full granary. He is a

Berry, balm to the bard, his father. Now Matthew
Ardent almond-tree, our
Regulus, small king, refreshes our eyes. In

Mirth we see the always-new miracle of time, strong
I-beam, holding up our house again, again
Thirteen years, 156 months, 4748 days our Matthew, our
Zygote, Rothenberg zareba, safe thicket that shields us
Velvet
Antlers budding
Holy, sweet as honey

VI

February 13, 1980

I read a review of something by "Madame X" yesterday. It is evil, her influence. She thinks she is making things better for the women to whom she is a kind of guru but it is all politics, THE MOVEMENT. First there was Marxism, when I was young, and you couldn't touch people except on that channel. Now there is this boring woman's movement and a mysticism is being made of some unexceptional demands and a whole surround of lesbianism and man-hatred has to be accepted along with demands that are strictly a *broitfrage*—a question of a piece of bread. I hate it. Many of my young friends are discovering that they do not want to let their fertile years pass by with no experience of childbearing and childrearing. It is almost too late for some of them when they turn from their hardwon careers toward their womanliness. The thing I find hard to swallow in "Madame X" is that her husband committed suicide and she has two or three sons. Why? Why is such as she given sons? It always comes back to that with me. *HaShem* must find me a terrible bore. A *noodnick* as the joke goes.

February 27, 1980

Yesterday I woke with a dream, which I made straight in the half-waking state as I awoke. I was with a group of poets, writers etc. They were holding eggs between their two palms. John Ashbery handed me an egg to hold, which he had been warming in his hands. It had a lovely color, sort of strawberry blond, like my Adam's coloring. My hands were quite warm and I held it until the shell came off. It was larger and had a dull surface but still that surprising strawberry-blond color unusual and lovely.

That disappeared and in my hands I held a newborn kitten of that color. I perceived that it needed a mother's care and I was distraught because I was not equipped to care for it. I made it a soft-cooked egg with beeftea and tried to dribble some into its mouth. It did not do. The kitten was treading my lap as it would its mother's, if it had one. I did not know what to do and I awoke slightly. In my half-waking state I was presented with, or found, a mother cat who had lost her kittens somehow. I rubbed the kitten, now in a weakened condition, against the cat's hind end — in order to make it smell like her own — and happily, she accepted it. She washed it thoroughly and it proceeded to nurse with much strength to the satisfaction of the mother cat and itself. It was a pale marmalade kitten with no stripes. Its pelt was thick. It was a beautiful fat kitten of a lovely color.

As I came fully awake I realized that the kitten was my poetry. John had passed it to me to hatch. I was not capable of making poetry. That is what I was telling myself. It was not a sad dream but a resigned one. I do not feel capability. The writing has been a natural, a bottom-line strength to me. I realize lately that I am not really of the company of writers and poets. I did not devote my life to it as they do. There is a real feeling of the work being what I was made for when I do work of this kind, but I have not given it first place in my life. It is a luxury to me not an absolute necessity. Earning a living, caring for others, caring for my house and garden have been.

July 8, 1980

Today I got a letter from C. who is M.'s new woman friend. She sounds uneasy with me. I suppose being presented to me by him in that way was not unlike meeting a mother-in-law for the first time. I'm sorry. Maybe it is her also, some way. It feels to me as if she could make M. happy and find a life for herself too in that. I hope so, fervently, for M.'s sake. Hers too. I told him he had to make a commitment to commitment not just to her, because every person has many faults, one as much as another. Endurance is all, to work it through and become snug in it like a worm in horseradish. To be at home in each other despite the bitterness. Right now they deny the possibility of anything but sweetness. The staying power is more important than the joy, I think.

Bonnefoy says in a poem "Threats of the Witness," "Now I've gotten old. Finally, the truth of the word and the truth of the wind have stopped their fight. The fire has gone out which was my church. I hardly have any more fear. I don't sleep."

I got a "credo" from A. yesterday. It was so young, so touching. I do love the effort my young friends put into becoming their true selves. He says the purpose of life is to live purposefully. He was educated by the Jesuits—a wonderful advantage. K., too is a person with deep capability for love and devotion. A good artist too.

"One can only sit by the window and pray," a woman with nine children once said to me when I asked her how she could bear it, since I found the fearful trembling over my one, almost insupportable. I do interfere more than is right. That comes from my terror and certainty of loss. Let these young ones (not so young in their own eyes) live well.

Yesterday N. and C. were here. They brought all kinds of marvelous cheeses, beautiful olives, and huge, natural grown tomatoes the like of which one sees for only one week during the year. The tomatoes have folds at the blossom end and a large rough navel with a bit of the thick, green stem still attached. The taste is of earth and sunlight. The *brokhas* come to mind. I say, "Blessed art Thou who hast brought forth the fruit of the vine or the fruit of the tree," with real enthusiasm. They brought, also, a kind of small wrinkled, black olive with lots of garlic, rosemary and thyme on it; sharp tasting, causing thirst for wine. Greek olives. We had melons and frozen fruit with vanilla iced milk. A day of wonderful human interaction, concrete tokens of affection, sunlight on the beach and simple sybaritic foods eaten together in friendship and communion.

Still, in a way they are like children who refuse wholesome food and eat the paint off the walls. They refuse the obvious turn toward happiness—which does take some trials, some sacrifice of present irresponsibility—and make themselves deeply unhappy. How I care for C. and wish he were my son.

But of course the wonderful thing for them and for us is that we are NOT their parents, yet the love from this age to that partakes of a lighter parental quality which is bearable, emollient, in its lightness.

DELAYED

I can see through three blocks of houses so
I will never die, she said, as she died.

The expression in Russian is different.
I can see three yards under where you stand.

Meaning: do not attempt to deceive me.
She maybe thought of death as deception,

I can see around corners. I see what?
Mud. I see a shadow on your kind face

When I mention his name. I thought he was
Your dear friend? He says about people that

He helped them get where they are. Why say that?
He talks too fast. He knows everybody.

He changes directions. He asks questions.
To which there are no answers because what

Is the question he really wants answered?
It all takes time and sharp focus. One must

Be as sharp as he is. This is not me
Since if I see three yards under your feet

I am stuck in the spring mud in my head
And if I see through three blocks of houses

I am distracted by what I see. Death.
Flink we would call him in Yiddish. Flicker.

He darts. What does he want? What is he at?
If you allow yourself to be screwed you

May find yourself with a future on which
You can not count. I love to count. I can

See three yards all around him, but not now.
Later I can tell it was a pig's foot

Sticky and not kosher. Later I can
Remember when it touched me. What? Besides

What he says, what does he want? And what is
He planning to do? I allowed myself

To get into this. I would like to know
If I am simple or devious. I

Know I am old and I try. I know what
I like, as they say, but is it true art?

KNOW ME AS I AM

With courage and heat his own
He became more than before
Surrounded all around
By princesses with long necks
And narrow hands

He served God gladly eleven days.
Powers above him
Sent him crawling, lusting
Dry and hot with need
For filth
At the same time
As he longed for better
And purer

Now nothing was nasty enough

When this passed he returned
To the vertical. He was himself
Up, up, like a rocking toy

"Please know me," he said
"Know me as I really am
I am a simple fellow
From time to time
I have these aberrations, alas

Oh, someone else in my skin
Takes over. Do not say it
Friendship, old friendships
Like bells, like buoys
Set me right

Let us be family people again
Let us go visiting
In the ordinary way
As if none of this
Had ever happened."

BREAK-UP

For Nina Yankowitz

You were always interested in place
most of all, even your parties.
I have discovered your low possibilities
your velleities. Come claim your stuff.
I am well rid of you.

We drove each other wild with our
different flags, but I
latched onto your constant longing
for blowing wind and sand.

Once your new body shone back at me
like the sun. Your lap was as if
covered with lace.
Do you remember the station
where we ate pancakes, where
the toilets groaned like a
mechanical trombone?
How we laughed together!
When lint falls on the air
I chew up the bed. Let me
tell you of my grassy plan
before all the snows of composition
press loud sobs out of you.
Put your chin on the sand.
Use your own hump for water
when you are thirsty. Get lost.
Oh now I question the value of dance
to the viewer. My tomorrow
is a moonlit cave. Vague!
Can a cow dance on the point of a parapet?
Not I!

THE FALL

In a space without gravity or light
They floated like large flecks of fire.
They did not fall.
The walls and ceiling took turns
Any wall could be up or down
       Divided in groups of three or five,
       Other numbers than two were engrossing,
       Because there was no more necessity.
In the lack of light their bones glowed
Like the top inch of a burning candle.
Their eyelids were moist
Always shining with expectation.
       They hung there for millenia, laughing
       Turned into milkmaids
       All smelled like kittens
       Stood with their heads together
       Their long braids touching.
"Ching," they tinkled like wind-chimes.
They were beginning to have breasts.
Anything was possible to them.
       They departed downward
       But nothing was up or down.
       Everything, Ching, was permitted.
       There was a EU there, as in euphoria.
       EU EU EU, they called to each other
       Let us play together.
       They burned honey-colored lights.
The place is not hot. There is no brimstone.
That is a common error.
The lights are large flecks of cold fire.
Nothing turns. Nothing has weight.

DIATRIBE FROM C BLOCK

No one asks what they were doing there in the first place.
Why were they in the Thuringian forest all gussied up anyhow?
Company after company in green and gold
And those excessively long swords?
Some money is in order too, up to a point.

Must. They have to. Not may, they must.
They were forbidden during certain hours.
Everybody knows they were not good at being forbidden.
That's why they were there, when you come down to it.
And parents, grandparents, sisters, brothers
May have been the cause of the vanity
Of seeing oneself so. And the presence
Of two hundred moist maidens was no help either
Dressed as they were in rose-colored scarfs, indeed!
No wonder they cheered.
For the purpose of regulation they had to cheer.
What else was there?

Suicide or escape. To deliver or try to deliver
Gifts or letters also forbidden. They were perishable.
Must travel a long way on consecutive days in long white robes
Must. The pleasures shortened in duration. Forbidden
If pleasing. Except to angelic escorts

WHO IS THIS STILLED

Who is this, stilled?
A knocking followed by silence.

Into the cup of our palms uplifted
The sparrows are falling like hail.

Time crouches in the dry leaves
Of your muttering.

Who were you, not animal, not child
Face smoothed away from us?

We try to enter the place you inhabit.
What warm place without bars

Has a spotted light for your blindness?
Where is a green freedom in which

Innocent bowels and bladder
May open at will?

Is there a cave underground, there beneath
With a constant supply of sweets
And kisses to comfort this root.

HEAL MY DREAMS

My dreams of myself, other people's dreams of me
Dreams of the dead with whom no dreamer may speak or eat
    or touch
Let them be healed

The empty plain, the dust, the greenish light, the dead forest
The kitten whose father has bitten off its head
The men with horsedicks, pulling broken shrimp out of
    their torn bellies
The white horse who clomps up the stairs saying my name
Looking for me in my bed

My work spoiled, my gifts rejected, one shoe always missing
The bed too short. The air, like tar, in which I try to swim
The gorilla of childhood who chases me up a barren hill
The monstrous babies with big heads, pale green, lavender
Who play beneath my window. The lizard rats I stab
With a huge fork repeatedly only to have them become whole
While I stab them

The paper boat which sinks beneath me as I stand in it
In a thin nightgown, leaving my knight in garnet armor
    on the shore

The sick dreams, the sad dreams, the dreams of terror
Let them be healed

FORBIDDEN MIXTURES I

Born from the earth, the earth-serpent
With its tail in its mouth, eats earth

One and an earth-serpent makes war
One and a sphinx is the death-riddle

The dragon's teeth, one by one
Are of the earth, are not two

One, they are one, and one, and warring
Warring, then dead. They are not true

Born from exactly the same
Or from totally different

Is too near or too far.
Two, not too near or too different

Are caring, are not walled in
Are not minotaured in

Mother and sister, father or brother
Are too near. The same is too near

Near blood is too dear
Born from two separates is more true

Two are right. True is right
Two are separate. Two separate ones

Born from the union of a man and a woman
Not born from earth as the plants grow

One you and the nearest is blind
Near blood is blind blood is not true

Two not too near are a good two
Two born from a man and a woman

214

Not born from the union with self
Not born from the earth-serpent

Born from like but not the same
Born to two who are near but not the same

Two from opposite sides of the fire
Two from either side of the circle

One and the same is lame
Is left-sided, is swollen-footed

One and itself is not true, is crookt
Born from the same is not the same

Born from itself is born from the earth
Is an earth-serpent, a sphinx, a minotaur

FORBIDDEN MIXTURES II

I am no organ, no name, no beatitude
But this faith roared home fresh.
I forget by Your company loss
And O so in sin made You do that.

My belief full, like a good-as-gold cow
I am more bad, too much I find
Who, if in a ditch and at fun, I am sin.
There is a demon in the fog
So low it neighs, mad to be let in
A doggy-smelling bum,

While a rose-sweetness adored, a name-day
A tithe in comely choir form
Tells me, "For light in day rob a morning
Core of the rose, old sigh, coil."

Is it dawn, rose-red in tan sun?
Is it mighty? Teach calm and do,
Spirit of my fathers, as a temper serious
I beg the Master to turn a bride.
Give a kiss in lamb-days.

Fills me more full than, O there!
Nicked in the attic. So I'll do right.
More mine as can be. Send no Greeks.

MY FAMILIAR

Benny comes to my door at irregular intervals
I do not know what brings him
I do not know what makes him stay away

"Benny," I say, "son of a Tzar, my beauty
Take a morsel in your mouth." He spits at me.

"Graf Pitosci," I say, "how are your extensive acres?"
He gives me a quick hit. He refuses my blandishments.

But he likes my errands. He knows that business.
He likes to take a toothache, cramps, backache
To the sourfaced neighbor nextdoor
Who keeps the boys' baseball if it gets into her yard.

BABA YAGA

Unpredictable as the three wishes
Granted by the little fish
To the fisherman

As difficult as ice-bound journeys
to the far north
She is their old world

Their Stonehenge, an endangered species
The witch in the wood, everybody's grandma
She tells long stories about dead relatives

The point of the story is at the end
Or the point is hidden between the lines
Barbed, and it hurts, like an infected splinter

The listeners must jump from meaning to meaning
They must take care. She is their history
Her closets are full of necessities

Pearly rings to go around the moon
Fields and spaces no one knows how
To get to anymore

ISLAND PRESENCE

Whenever someone from the islands
Tells you how to cook something
With achiote in it
She meets your eyes and says
With no emotion showing

For the color only

But when I cook with red annato seed
My house has a heavy presence
And if any island person passes by my door
Our eyes meet
And I say with a straight face

I fried some red annato in the oil first
A little—for the color only

And we nod

THE WITCH LEONARDO

The two sides of an arch
Make from their two weaknesses
One strength.
If one side were removed
The arch would crash.

The sorcerer Volkh
Could change into a white bull
A bright falcon, a grey wolf, an ant.

The strongest man in the world, Svyatagor
Tried to lift a small cloth bag
From the earth. He pulled so hard
He found himself two feet into the earth
The blood rushing from his nose and mouth.
He died without moving the little bag.

Volkh, the Volga, is a sorcerer.
He is part of the moist earth.
A white bull with gold horns
A bright falcon, a grey wolf, a tiny ant
He treads on earth, flies over her, burrows within.
He is part of an arch with the earth.

Svyatagor, the strongest man in the world
Thinks his strength the whole arch.
"The force desired to subdue its cause
When this is subdued, it destroys itself."
So said Leonardo, who knew.

LITTLE BOY WITCH

Little fox-face in a thicket
Will not come up my high steps
For a cup of water

They have lost their way
They say, with simple flesh
And innocent eyes

Whose way this is *he* knows
So he carries my paper cup away
With his valuable tooth in it

Which has just come out
And he has a use for it
As I have too

SAND-BOX THEOLOGY

I think he's the nicest Man in the world

My father says there's no such Person

Then who made you?

My father planted a worm and it grew

Something makes it grow
Some die and do not grow

There is Nobody there
I'm sure. I know

If He can be here
He can be there
That's how I know
He's everywhere

No. It isn't so
You have to plant a seed
The rain makes it grow

RETURN—A SPELL

Father, father
Dig me up
Turn me around
Let me return

Mother, snug and fitting mother
Turn me around
Push me out

Water, water
Living water
Turn me over
Flow me out

Out of the well from which
I was drawn
Back to the source
From which I arose

Turn, turn. Let me return
Return to the pit
From which I was dug

THE RUINED FARMHOUSE

There is a pool by the cellar covered with the greenest algae.
Someone glides by making a breeze through the
    bachelor-buttons
Flowering myrtle, gill-over-the-ground, blue gentians.
She sighs for the brothers all missing because of her.
The children scattered to Texas, to California.

She used to put up jars and jars of beans, carrot pickles
    in turmeric.
There was a five-apple tree by the kitchen door with
    Yellow Transparents.
She made cider for the ones who are gone using the little
    cider press.
She'd let the raw cider ferment in the barn. After a week or two
It would freeze solid because up here there were two seasons
Winter and July. For Thanksgiving she would go out to the
    barn and
Pierce a hole in the hard-frozen cider. From deep in the center
She would drain off the apple-jack, more than a hundred proof
A lovely, light golden color, smelling of apple harvest.

Now there is only a rectangular cement pit where the cellar was
And a tall brick chimney still standing.
There is a rotten peach tree with greenmoldy fruit.

Down below is the Cherry Valley Creek with a fine stand of
    oats in front.
Where did all the Joe-Pye Weed come from so thick and red?
Who planted the tiger-lilies all over the bank beneath the
    five maples?

Upstairs in the house there was rose-patterned wallpaper.
There were homemade toys there and a little window
    overlooking the creek.

The red cow used to come and look in the kitchen window in
   the evening.
The children laughed, shrill with relief that it was only the cow.
There was an outhouse back there with a heart-shaped vent
   over the door.
In the bigger bedroom upstairs there was a Jenny Lind bed
Short, with hand-turned bars. It was good for making love.
The frames of the windows and the baseboards and lintels
   were of hardwood.
The floors in the room with the baywindow were of eight inch
   cherrywood planks.

The wind-break hedge of cypress behind the house is
   grown up into trees.
The peonies and raspberries in front of the barn are choked
   with tall weeds.

She lies buried in her dark place under the hedge.

RAPE OF THE BUTTERFLY WEED

Odd-colored weed, sceptre
attended by monarchs
cluster of apricots
brassy cauliflower
bloom for me.

Buck with seven antlers
lifted in air
reluctant arriver
Joseph-flower
gold-eyed dreamer
grow for me

When I dug you out
where you hid
in dark leaves glowing with spite
you left your cloak in my hand
it poisoned my nights.
Pleurisy root
bloom now for me.

AMULET AGAINST DROUGHT

Wet tongue of a young male dog
Free on a fine morning

Wet leaves of a violet
Tear on the cheek of a just-loved woman

Tumbling of water over small stones
Rustle of poplar leaves

Steam above a cup of tea
Smell of cut grass, wet

Mourning dove drinking
Its beak down, then up, drinking

Drop, drop, one at a time
One by one

Drought be sated. Dry be wet.
Udder be full. Cloud be full

River be overflowing
Dry be wet

Wet be present. Wave be wet
Hush, be wet. Rush be wet

Not overmuch, not overmuch
But well up, fall down. Rain

Dew, mist, heavy cloud, come
Drop, drop. Come together. Rain.

AMULET AGAINST SLANDER

Metzorah, Thazria
Molds, plague of parasites

Catch a mouse
Slit its eyes, say

"Go into the mouse
Go into the mouse."

Poke the slanderer with a sharp pin.
Show her the blood on the pin

Hide behind the door of her hallway
Watch her come in out of the dark

Gather the dust of her pathway
Scatter it under a tree

AMULET AGAINST CANCER

Big black dog
Who lives away from masters

I growl back at you
Wild dog with no master

I advance slowly
One step at a time

I hit you between the ears
On top of the head

With a wooden spoon
I spit in your face

Then feed you
You must live in my house

In a corner. You must learn
How to live in my house
With me

LUCK'S DAUGHTER

The serpent-shaped daughter of Luck
Who lay with her father before she was born
Who rubbed on his hump from inside
The ophidian daughter enters my house

She unbuttons my sternum, I do not feel it
Slides a light hand under my ribs
Now I'm missing my heart beat
The many-hued daughter of Luck

Has stolen some parts of the rainbow
Some rays of the sun, the light of my eyes
In a casual drawer at home she has dropped
A single gold earring, my eyes

A dead mouse, a piece of green money
Rags caked with blood and a few dusty
Beats of my heart, that magpie daughter
That obdurate daughter of Luck

EIGHTH STREET SATURDAY NIGHT

In this place steeled against rip-offs
A praying mantis, dusty
And a brownskin girl, smiling

They break holes in the concrete
They are meteors, ozone
Distracting the pushers and pimps

All the fools buying it
Rubbing their dead faces

SHE LAUGHED

The rat
Ate half the herring
The children
Would not eat it

It was good food
She said
The rat
Would not touch it
If it were
Not good

She laughed
At the empty cupboards
At the rat
Who bit
The baby's nose

At the charm
Like Harry's
Of her daughter
A milk-greedy whore

At eight
Who lay with the milkman
In the milkwagon
For free milk
A man older
Than Harry

She laughed
At the holes
In the kitchen floor
She sweated
And burned
For Harry
And laughed
While he plied the Atlantic
Gambling on liners

She sweated and burned
For Harry
His fine hands
And moustaches
His return
From the liners
With love
Food and laughter
Til he left
To his art
And his wife in England

She was pregnant again
And laughing
Feverish breathing fast
And sweating
For Harry
She died laughing
For Harry

LONELINESS OF THE GOLEM

When the hand moves
When it lives for its own need
When it lights on an object
Like a magician's hand
To make things disappear

Then the will of the hand
Separated from the head
From the warmth of the person
Is a punishment
A true punishment

When they cut the hand off
In times gone by
It relieved the whole
Of the need to consider
The solitude of the hand
Separated from its person

To be driven to this act
Headlong, alone
Enrages the hand
Turns the being to stone
The face to brass

The hand separated, alone
Light as a dandelion seed
Wandering acquisitive
Needs a family, a community
To return to the whole

A band of murderers
A den of thieves
Return the hand
Light and skillful
To the ordinary

WHEELS

for Elena
1950-1977

It's their quickness
The way they pay attention
To the part that counts
Without really knowing
The whole thing
Through and through

And what they do to grammar
How they return to the logic underneath.

Then, their feet are so enthusiastic.
They open their mouths so wide
On fresh air or sunlight
Even rain or snow

       But now they have been won over
       Convinced rather, by four wheels, three, or two.
       Still, they take them as another kind of growth
       Which is their main preoccupation anyhow.
       They roar around the block after each other
       Crashing like uprooted trees

       While those who made them cell by cell
       Spoonful by spoonful, lie in the dark
       Turning from side to side like off-center wheels
       Feeling thrifty, stingy even, with the long work
       That brought these small shouters this far
       And—may it not be so—no further
       Because when together with their own small species
       They may fly off, unpredictable, to disintegration
       Bright-faced with exhilaration.

WAITING

To get through quicken the clocks on the wall
Waiting for woe to end for calm to stay
Breathe less. Do not blink. Prevent the beat
Look far away. Ignore the swing of the sun

Sit with your spout pouring nothing
Waiting for pain to end for an end to
Longing do not cut your hair or change
Your clothes. Be without your body. Quiet

Your skin. Turn off the lights. Waiting for months
To be empty, your own, repeat old names
Polish pennies scrub stones. Slow the hands
Of your water clock the clock of yourself

I TRIED

I planned tomorrow bright, inside.
Beat on the door with fist and two left feet.
I filed the waste away. Again I tried

With bribes and smiles, the stubborn doorman, Pride.
To get within just once, who cared, I'd cheat.
I planned tomorrow bright. Inside

I pushed with thrust for Fame. To earn the right
Then begged and showed my wounds out in the street.
I filed the waste away again. I tried

To ease their pains—Oh cure mine too, I cried—
Compared with which my troubles were a treat.
I planned tomorrow bright inside.

I cancelled grandma, smothered baby, killed a bride,
Then turned with broken heart to Mercy's seat.
I filed the waste away. Again? I tried

Without trying. I looked around outside,
Found the walls all breached, no need to beat.
I planned tomorrow. Bright inside
I filed the waste away. Again. I tried.